S0-CFP-320

The Secret Music
of the Soul

IMAGINE RECORDS & PUBLISHING
C.P. 2442
Ste Adèle
Québec, CANADA
J0R 1L0

Author's photograph: Michel Legendre

English translation: Hélène Pallascio & Brenda O'Brien

Original title: "Les secrets de la musique de l'âme"
Published by Les Éditions & Disques Imagine

First edition

Legal deposit: 2nd quarterly 1991

NATIONAL LIBRARY OF CANADA
BIBLIOTHÈQUE NATIONALE DU QUÉBEC

ISBN 2-9801966-1-4

ALL RIGHTS RESERVED FOR ALL COUNTRIES

Patrick Bernhardt

The Secret Music
of the Soul

ACKNOWLEDGMENTS

I wish to thank France Lortie for her work on preliminary drafts and for her careful and attentive listening; thank you to Joanne Cyr for her advice and to Denis Bernier for his proofreading expertise; thanks also to Yves Ducharme for giving me access to reference books and providing assistance.

I wish to express my gratitude to Pierre A. Durivage for his trust and his professionalism.

Finally, my thanks to all those who have contacted me through the Atlantis Angelis Network and who are wholehearted witnesses to the merit of my work and my research.

P.B.

The Atlantis Angelis Network
Patrick Bernhardt
C.P. 2442
Ste-Adèle
Quebec, Canada
J0R 1L0

To my Masters

"Strengthened by the power of sound, we happily make our way through the somber night of death"

Mozart, *The Magic Flute*

"While nuclear physicists clearheadedly examine their facts and theories in light of the conceptual approaches of mystics, many biologists and doctors limit themselves to the confines of their reductionist dogmas."

Étienne Guillé
(Ph.d., Professor of Mathematics, researcher and lecturer at the University of Paris' Molecular Biology Department.)

CONTENTS

CHAPTER 2
THE POWER OF SONG
AND WORDS   81

TO THE READER

AN INVITATION TO A JOURNEY

I am neither a materialist nor a spiritualist. I have always been "between" designations, between states. For this reason, most of the time scientists consider me to be religious, and the religious consider me to be an atheist... For what purpose? Nothing. Nothing, if not perhaps to observe the beauty of the great white clouds travelling across the sky and to remember that only change is changeless and to imagine that this contemplation will be, for each of us, in itself, an answer. For the very nature of the world of forms and names around which we gravitate forces the mind to put a label on everything. On things, as well as on beings.

I am not a musicologist, nor even a "real" musician in the classic sense of the term, and much less am I a doctor. I sing, I search; I observe the effects of the voice on the body, of vowel sounds on the mind, of music on people. All in all, nothing complicated. Some things I do understand, others, as it often happens, I do not understand. I am simply a traveller in search of a better world.

My interest in phonic formulae with profound vibrational effects, "mantras", stems from an experience that happened in 1977 while I was practising the "Japa", that is to say, the rhythmic repetition of a mantra. Every individual, without exception, can live through the same experience I have. It corresponds to what the *Mandukya Upanishad* (part of the Vedic Scriptures) describes as:

"the fourth state which involves neither inner knowledge, nor exterior knowledge, nor knowledge of one, nor of the other, nor global knowledge, which is at one and the same time neither knowledge nor unknowledge; which is invisible, elusive, unthinkable, unnamable, whose essence is but the experience of one's own Self, which counters diversity, which is appeased, benevolent, devoid of duality, which is the Self, the object of Knowledge."

I have set out on this journey, this quest towards inner music, simply by trying to relive this experience, to understand it, to come to terms with it, to attend to it, and eventually to describe it, so joyous, free, spontaneous and unforgettable is its very nature.

As often as possible, I avoid places and books where a great number of "ism" words appear; they are often very far from the truth, like fanaticism, for instance.

I am fascinated by the power of words, of music and of vibrations in general. My quest towards the origins of language has brought me to Sanskrit, the mother of all languages, put into writing 5,000 years ago. Sanskrit words therefore appear here and there in my text; their definitions are found in the glossary included in the final pages of this book.

On my way, I might just as easily have discovered the ancient Aztec language or even Hebrew, or perhaps the hieroglyphic language of the Pharaohs...

Truth is one and belongs to no one person in particular. No one culture, no one tradition, as brilliant as it may be, can claim to possess Truth without falling prey to error....and ridicule. Truth is not static, it is in a constant state of evolution. Its essence remains the same, but its aspects are infinite. And so, it is impossible to "find" it or to understand it intellectually.

All that is possible for us, provided we have truly desired it, is to one day feel the profound joy of perceiving or experiencing its countless facets; this in itself constitutes an initiation of sorts. Therefore, this is but a shared experience and not an attempt to "preach" the truth.

All those who preach have something in common: they believe that they are right and all others, it follows, are wrong. This is an amusing point of view and one that, after all, can be respected. The danger here is that this point of view leads directly to...inquisition. And it can safely be said that in today's world, inquisition – whether from the media or in political or medical circles – is still a very sore point in the minds and hearts of those obstinately closed to the new dimensions of art, freedom and health!

Therefore, I am not seeking to convince anyone with lofty pseudo-scientific theories and elaborate hypotheses. All that I endeavour is to simply extend an invitation. An invitation to an inner celebration whose principal activity is being happy.

Do not be misled by my use of the words soul, sacred, divine, absolute, etc. Things need a name and the human language has its limitations. Reality goes far beyond our written symbols even if, as we will see later, they can be considered as "passwords" and even though they provide access to a type of image of the invisible spheres.

Of course, these words would not be used in psychoanalysis, because for the intellect, they belong to the realm of uncertainty. Rather, one would refer to "the source of subconscious images or dreams", to "the organizational centre from which emanate regulatory effects and which seems to be a 'nuclear atom' in our psychic system" or something of the sort... in short, one would use the intellect in formulating references.

More simply stated, Carl Jung calls this centre "the self". In naming this intimate inner space, I preferred to choose the word "soul" and the word "divine" because I find them poetical and they speak to my heart. Throughout the ages, human beings have been intuitively aware of the existence of such a centre. The Greeks called it "daïmon", in Egypt it was expressed by the concept of "Basoul", the Romans named it the "spirit" inherent in each individual. The ancient Vedic civilization knew it as the "atma", the indestructible lifeforce, the basis of each person, eternally in harmony with universal precepts.

So I have invented nothing. My only effort is to shed new light on this centre hidden in the furthest corners of human history, to reactivate, to some extent, this inner space of peace and light occulted by the modern world's speed and the degree of technology it depends on, both of which conspire against it, without even knowing why.

If such an inner place exists, one ought to be able to reach it, or at least to perceive it, to feel it. And yes, it is possible to do so.

By listening closely, one can even hear sounds, frequencies, songs, waves, wonderful harmonics which spring forth spontaneously

17

from this magical space found in our deepest, innermost selves and nowhere else.

Once, through a process or another, all these acoustic vibrations dance together in perfect alliance and unite their "voices" in perfect equilibrium, it is then possible for us to sense an admirable and sublime melody which goes beyond the strictly physical senses.

This music is played to the rhythms of grace and love; of the absolute love, pure and unconditional, that only universal life has the privilege of knowing.

> Healing is the Goal
> Sincerity is the Force
> Universal vibration is the Tool
> Second Birth is the Fruit

P.B.

INTRODUCTION

IN SEARCH OF THE MUSIC OF THE SOUL

"All is vibration, nothing is inert, everything vibrates; all things achieve balance through compensating oscillations."

Hermes

"Provided he can rid himself of his rigid educational baggage, each human being feels that there is an undeniable reality, no matter how difficult it may be to detect. But what may remain mystic for a moment is not, for all that, unconceivable. One must be moved by a steadfast faith to dare to precisely and firmly express what science considers as a pleasing poetic vision. Yet how many times has this vision preceded by millennia, by centuries or by decades the experimental proof which is in fact a late-coming verification of what has already been revealed by seemingly fantastic premonitions. The scientist is afraid to recognize the poet within him for fear of being cast out by his peers. But the scientific researcher who lacks any form of poetry is the epitome of the utterly sterile scientist who nevertheless contributes by asserting with his measurements and statistics what the poet has already perceived."

Father Alfred Tomatis
La Nuit utérine (The Uterine Night)

"If it is not to fail, our effort to formulate reality into thought must include all that has been acquired through modern science."

Hubert Reeves, astrophysicist
The Time for Elation
Does the universe have a meaning?

Imagine

Just imagine a wonderful healer who has the power to eliminate gradually everything that congests your cells, that impedes the proper functioning of your organs, that slows down the blood circulation in your arteries. Imagine that freedom, that lightness...

Imagine he has the power to soothe your nerves, to relax your muscles, to strengthen your vertebrae and to massage deeply your back and your shoulders extremely gently, confidently and benevolently.

Imagine that for you, his hands and his voice are healing hands and a soothing voice.

Imagine further that this healer has the power to pierce the secrets of the aura surrounding you and that he can illuminate your aura by softly withdrawing all limitations, fears, blocks, worries, conflicts, problems that have been stored away since adolescence, childhood, birth and even beyond, since the evolutions and experiences of previous lives.

Imagine the absence of fear, of negativity, the return of confidence and the sense of absolute security which arises from an intimate relationship, a confidential complicity with nature and the qualities of the true self.

Imagine that this healer fills you with light and joy and that this light brightens your thoughts and makes each of your cells smile.

Imagine further that he extends an invitation to you and gives you the power to propel yourself, to project yourself in space with your astral body, on the wings of your own creative visualization, as far as the most beautiful gardens of the universe, as far as the crystal spheres where our cousins of the stars reside, who with us shape networks of clarity and who visit us periodically on their galactic spacecrafts, propelled by the winds of unconditional love for the greatest pleasure of all creation.

Imagine total relief, complete self-liberation from all negative tensions which make us doubt beauty and life's eternity.

Imagine that freedom from these tensions has not only the power to heal you, but that it also holds the power to awaken in you something absolute, something immortal.

Imagine, lastly, that this extraordinary magician really exists and introduces himself to you through the simple form of musical energies from a higher realm, with the objective of soothing, healing and raising the whole of humanity to an existence marked by eternity, consciousness and genuine well-being.

These few words will only provide you with a brief glimpse of the images and the symbols, of the inspirations and motivations of the work you hold in your hands. Yet we all bear within us these symbols and images, deeply hidden in the recesses of our heart, whatever our cultural, traditional, social or religious persuasions.

I wish you an excellent journey towards the limitless plains of the inner gardens, in search of the soul and its heavenly music. Dan Millan once said: "Knowledge alone is not sufficient; it does not have a heart." Travellers in search of the music of the soul are therefore invited not to burden themselves with the heavy baggage of preconceived ideas which prevent the free circulation of intuitive energies and are at the origin of the limits of the so-called scientific integrity of the rationalist school of thought. "The mind is like a parachute; it functions only when opened", and so it is with the heart. It is with an open mind and heart that one can perceive the superior intuitions and intimate revelations which constitute the "Open, Sesame!" of all sincere seekers. The symbolic resonant formula can then lighten the whole being by unveiling to it the mysteries of its origin, of its cosmic identity, of its destiny.

An ever-present energy

Our nervous system is constantly submitted to the torture of the modern world's discordant noises. Unless we happily reside in a place where nature's song has been preserved, day and night our ears are literally pierced by the devastating and deafening uproar of the mechanical exploitation of matter. Internal combustion engines, howling sirens, shrill whistles, exasperating grinding noises gradually ruin our body and mind. Moreover, what we laconically call music in our current consumer system is sometimes the unconscious echo of the noisy machines that surround us.

At the dawn of the Aquarian era, machine-like vibrations, distortions and shrieks all too often replace the melodies and harmonies proper to genuine music. The spoken word itself, a unique gift which makes the human race the rightful heir to superior energies *(para prakriti)*, is often used to achieve negative ends, without any consideration and in almost total ignorance of the awesome power it holds. Can one grasp to what extent the cumulative effect of these noises and statements, often saturated by nihilism and negativity, can devastate our inner space? Can one picture how many illnesses, disorders, suicides and maladjustments these sound energies can provoke? It is precisely in an attempt to heal these wounds that this new era's composers have the mission of developing a type of music likely to heal the wounds caused by the plague of modern times: noise. More than a simply relaxing music, it is in sound itself that these new composers set out on their search for a music of transformation. To transform anxiety into tranquility, fear and anguish into a sense of plenitude and trust, inert obscurity into vivid light, pain into serenity: such is the fundamental intention injected into their creations. The source of inspiration and choice of sounds therefore place the listener in an exceptional atmosphere, profoundly different from all he has known before, where the feeling of completeness is not artificially imposed on the mind, but quite to the contrary, where it is an ever-present energy that has been there for a very long time, which has always been there, which he can find again effortlessly as long as this positive energy comes not from the outside, but from his inner self.

Furthermore, these musical energies have a tendency to carry the listener who listens profoundly to a supra-natural atmosphere, peaceful and happy, one that is imperceptible to the ear that is not anointed with the balm of unconditional love. This world, unperceived by the physical eye and ear (but which it is possible to perceive on one hand, through the penetrating observation of the sacred texts known in the world, and on the other hand, through one's own intuitions and transpersonal experiences) corresponds to the one and multiple reality of the altered states of consciousness. At this level, everything is possible; everyday stress disappears, worries and tensions evaporate and the listener penetrates into the sphere of his own serenity. In that sphere, all his senses are captivated by a unique pleasure and he finds that this pleasure is within him. At this point, the keys of the universe are in his hands. He need only leave the doors of his heart and mind wide open for terrestrial and celestial harmony to provide him with the opportunity of living the intense life of his dreams.

Atlantis Angelis: a simple testimony

The origin of the present work is the musical piece entitled Atlantis Angelis, presented to the public under the title "Self-healing mantras sung in Sanskrit". While listening to these sound vibrations many people sense a special form of energy and experience certain transformations at the psychic and physical levels. Some listeners even speak of a spiritual dimension and an inner opening-up towards the world they perceive within themselves, a world to which they gain access through these sound vibrations. As an example, allow me to quote a beautiful letter written by Ms Nicole Blanchette, who orients her research work towards the practice of evolutionistic dance in which the spiritual approach and artistic spirit tend to merge:

> "This is simply a testimony of my ten years' experience in research, as completed and revealed through the support of Atlantis Angelis. On the very first listening, this music led me to the lifeforce which allowed me to finalize my approach to evolutionistic dance. During all these years of research – a journey which brought me to creativity and which led me to

question – I listened intently to different music in order to tame within it the inner dance which cleans, activates fields of energy and harmonizes by bringing us to the very heart of the current which lies beneath our lifeforce. Strengthening and awakening people would help the planet fulfill its destiny. But how to raise consciousness and awaken even more the inner song within each of us, how to bring ourselves to find inside us peace, love, intuition and liberation from the strongest ego attacks which often lead to illness. Movements of the body, temple of the soul; music of the soul, the rhythms of life: two entities essential to the creation of one's own space where peace, harmony, and love of self and of all the cosmos reigns. It seemed that time was passing so quickly and I saw that in this life, I would not succeed in composing the music that would be enlightening enough to help people reach the soul's most important vibrations. In my eyes, it seemed that this task had been entrusted to another soul, one that I would undoubtedly meet one day. This friend in the invisible plain would cross my path... And this friend is *Atlantis Angelis*."

Each week it is my pleasure to receive encouraging letters from those who believe in higher vibrational music and who confirm the cogency of my research. So it is with this second, movingly sincere testimony, provided by Ms Jeanne d'Arc Xavier, a phytotherapeutic nurse specializing in alternative medicine:

"With your beautiful music, you have the capacity of building temples in people's hearts. Through its strong magnetic power, I can sense that each listener is transformed and bettered. This music brings me something undefinable and marvellous."

Finally, I would like to quote a few sentences from the Montreal Saï Baba Yoga Centre's moderator, Marie Loranger, who wrote the following to me:

"On Saturday, April 15, I was browsing in an esoteric bookshop when suddenly the matchless beauty of the Atlantis Angelis theme filled the air. I paused attentively and silently and drank at its source. After a while I left, bringing with me the priceless treasure of your beautiful music. Only when evening fell could I listen to it once again, in the silence of the night. I cannot describe the deep emotion I felt. No language exists to express what I experienced. Beyond my control, tears of joy streamed from my eyes and along my face, like lively streams of water, and I felt purified of all sadness and worry. A song of bliss sprang from my soul and a wave of tenderness overwhelmed me totally. I felt the vibrations of the purest regions of my soul. With immense gratitude my heart swelled for such music, the music of the soul, genuine light. I cried out: Lord! Is it possible that on this suffering earth, so torn by the lack of love, there exists a music so transparent that Your living beauty flows through it as from the purest spring? My experience was one of genuine communion. These moments have deeply marked me. I felt that I was seeing myself for the very first time. The emotion that *Atlantis Angelis* brings to me is a quivering of the soul, a love song, a vibrating symphony, and beings of the highest levels – the devas, the angels, the deities and all spirits – must surely have been moved by this music's infinite tenderness. To listen to it is to welcome your own soul into your hands. It is to feel a profound joy. Its love vibrations will elevate the vibrational frequency of the planet and hearts will feel less pain.''

These testimonies are quoted because they are self-explanatory. They represent the burning admissions of people who have succeeded in slightly lifting the veil of infinite mystery. By letting musical energies take effect within themselves, attentively and consciously, they have been able to feel and experience something profound and unforgettable. Illusion? Sentimentality? Unreal impression? False belief? Unhealthy sensitivity? Or truth and the perception of a superior reality?

Setting out on an adventure

It is precisely to answer these questions that I invite you to set out on an adventure in search of the music of the soul. During this journey, we will see in the universe of sounds in what measure sound in general – and music in particular – affects living organisms, which experiences have been conducted in the past and which can be attempted at home. This penetration into the mystic world of music will show us how humans and the societies they build are subject to the secret influence of the musics their societies nourish themselves on. Then we will examine the very power of the spoken word. Is it possible that the simple fact of asserting something through the sound of words could lead us to its manifestation? Is it possible that the music of words holds the mysterious power of facilitating the crystallization, in us and in our environment, of the nature and qualities of our assertions? Such are the questions which will be answered in the first two chapters.

The third chapter will be devoted to the energy of mantras. What is a mantra? Do the Christian, Moslem, Buddhist, Jewish, and Judaic religious systems have their own prayer-mantras? How does the energy of mantras function? For all of these questions, we will attempt to find an answer together. The mantras' way will lead us naturally to the strange phenomenon of the "Sacred Names" and we will attempt to establish the sovereignty of these spiritual chants and their great power of purification by using as a source of reference the *Puranas*, the most ancient scriptures known on Earth, quoting as proof the analytical reports of the great scholars of the soul. Fundamentally, this meditation on the Sacred Names will be universal in quality, and we will take a close look at the prayers and the glorification of the Holy Names as they are presented to humanity by all the great traditional movements known on the planet.

Chapter Four will deal with the inconceivable energy and the mysterious powers related to the chanting and listening of the spiritual and absolute sound vibrations. We will consider the possibility of a direct relationship with the soul of the universe, achieved by singing its countless Names. We will subsequently see how this relationship becomes a unique oasis where the living being can quench his thirst for infinite love. All that will be left for us to do then will be to proceed with practice and the fifth chapter will explain how to immerse oneself into an all-consuming musical bath. Repeated references to authoritative works on the topic will assist us in this task.

Finally, we will consider how the music of the Aquarian Age can help humanity through the crisis it faces today and how composers and listeners can participate in this extraordinary planetary renewal process, this wonderful transformation of societies and of consciousnesses which we are spectators of now and henceforth, actors and channels through which a new people of light is currently being born.

Rediscovering the energetic dimension of sounds

In the modern world, most musical vibrations that reach us have the disadvantage of making us forget why we were born to Earth:

to evolve. It seems that in each era, most musical productions were created solely for a purely aesthetical purpose, or merely for their stimulating effect and that today still, the spiritual essence of sounds is relegated to the background, if not ignored altogether. It is this realization which led Beethoven to say to Betina Brentano in the course of a conversation:

> "Just as thousands of people enter into marriage for love and just as love is not revealed to them even once, although in a way each of them do practise it, thousands are involved with music without ever touching upon its revelations."

In general, we are interested only in the exterior side of sounds; form is often perceived as more important than essence. But this music of form, devoid of the "inner spark of the fire of the spirit" provides only meagre nourishment and holds no power to raise the soul beyond the human condition. In a way, it is a sophisticated shell but one that is hollow and without substance. It addresses either our senses, exciting us, or our minds, moving us; at times, it addresses our intelligence by giving us the illusion of vague intellectual pleasure. All this provokes tension and stress. Seldom do harmonies directly address the soul, that is to say the immortal lifeforce. Our aim, then, will be to rediscover the energetic dimension of sounds, the transforming power and the true function of musical energies. We will attempt to enlighten the conscience with the eternal power of sounds and will demonstrate how, by the use of his own essence as score and instrument, along with the composer and the performer, the listener becomes the music's third creator. At this level, musical science is useless and only an extremely strongly directed power of concentration is genuinely effective. By identifying perfectly with the music and by conversing with it as with a human being, the listener will be privy to revealing answers which liberate him from the weight of his existential problems and lead him to inner illumination.

Intellect and revelation

What is the music of the soul? To give a satisfactory answer to this question, one should first ask: what is the soul? This question amounts to asking: who are we? We are confronted here with the age-old "who am I?" and the well-known "know thyself" of the greatest thinkers of our times. Answering the question "what is the soul" is a major undertaking which in itself would require several volumes of writing. However, it is possible to succeed in finding an answer much more rapidly by leaving aside, on the one hand, all intellectual speculation and on the other hand, by attempting to awaken inner intuition by turning to the authoritative writings of theosophic research (From the Greek: theosophia: illuminism which has the objective of union with the Divine principle).

Let us see what is hidden in this small word "soul". For Latin peoples, the anima, the soul, is the very breath of life. However, there have always been atheists or nihilists on Earth who do not believe in its existence. Giono said of one of them "that he no longer felt sure of the immortal quality of his soul".

When he began to believe that his reason and his intellect were the perfect tools for his search of truth, the human being lost his knowledge of the soul. He let his intuition die. Such is the tragedy of the world, which attempts to comprehend the broad expanse of the ocean by comparing it to the "reasonable" dimensions of a well... How absurd it is to try to measure the unlimited with a limited instrument!

Basarab Nicolescu, a great scientific analyst, remarked:

> "Idolatry of the intellect alone inevitably leads to mutilation and destruction (perhaps less visible on the individual level, but how much rampant on the social level)."

Hence, let us forget the intellect for a moment and let us simply seek the information we need in theosophical research and from revelation. Why seek a source of reference in the most important and best-known scriptures – biblical, Buddhist, Koranic and particularly *Vedic Scriptures*? What is a revealed scripture? What are the *Vedic*

Scriptures? How can the *Vedic Scriptures* help us in our research into the human soul? Revelation is the action of suprasensitive forces which provide humankind with the knowledge of realities its intellect is unable to discover by itself. Does this fall into the realm of religion? No. Revelation is of the free and simple realm of "direct experience". It is the experience of grace as perceived directly.

The Vedic Scriptures: a bridge over oblivion

The word *Vedic* means knowledge. The Vedic verses are often quoted as references in this book, therefore it is essential to visualize accurately what they represent. *Vedic* is a Sanskrit word. Its Sanskrit roots can be interpreted in several different ways, but in fact, the profound meaning of the word is "knowledge". These texts are not, as many believe, Scriptures peculiar to India; their teaching is universal. Were we to study them attentively, we would see that Vedic standards are all justified.

The *Vedic Scriptures* are also described as "*srutis*", a word signifying knowledge acquired from a model entity, that is to say a person free from duality and able to transmit knowledge without modifying or altering it. The *srutis* are compared to a mother. If a child wants to know who his father is, he must ask his mother. If she tells him that a given person is his father, he has no other choice but to take her word since he has no other means of finding out the truth... Similarly, to know what surpasses our capacity to understand and perceive, we can trust the *Vedic Scriptures* if we so wish. Vedic knowledge is passed on from master to disciple. If we try to acquire perfect knowledge through our own experience, we may possibly succeed, but to save time, it is possible to adopt this method. Let us remember, however, that we bear truth within us; the "hidden master" (*caitya-guru*), strong and subtle energy ensconced in all individuals, can transmit to us the knowledge of invisible things through the intermediary of the Buddhi (higher intuition).

According to the *Upanishads*, the universe is holographic. All that emanates from the Whole is also a whole. Scriptures are therefore completely useless to an entity who has been awakened to reality. Born of the universal Oneness, we bear within us universal truth. Therefore, while this potential genuinely exists, it is often latent, unexploited. Left to itself, the intuitive inner source can be awakened, among other things, by the revealed text.

In this way, the *Vedic Scriptures* are useful as revelation tools. Vedic information is for us a means of remembering what has always been but what we have chosen to forget. Revealed scripture represents a bridge over oblivion, the possibility of attaining a different level of consciousness.

What is the soul?

What do the *Vedic Scriptures* say on this topic? According to the *Bhagavad-Gita*, what penetrates the entire body cannot be annihilated and it shares in a suprasensitive energy inconceivable to reason and the senses. Nothing can destroy this essence. **The soul is the vital principle of the body it inhabits.** The *Svetasvatara Upanishad* even reveals its esoterical dimensions: a ten-thousandth of the breadth of a hair. The distinct soul would therefore be a spiritual atom, finer than material atoms. They exist in an infinite number. This minute spark is the vital principle of the physical body, where its influence spreads everywhere. Consciousness manifests itself by exercising its influence throughout the entire body and it is the proof of the soul's existence, the latter being its source. Deprived of consciousness, the physical body is a lifeless object. It follows then that consciousness springs from the soul and not from some combination of chemical elements. The *Mundaka Upanishad* specifies:

> "Perfect intelligence can accept the soul, whose dimensions are infinitely small. It floats, supported by five types of air (*prana, apana, vyana, samana* and *udana*). Located in the heart, it distributes its energy to the whole body. Once purified from the contamination of these five types of air, it reveals its inconceivable power." (mund. 111.19)

31

Materialist scientists claim that the soul is non-existent, **only** because their pettiness prevents them from using their power of observation!

Yet, over the course of millennia, many *yogis* have succeeded in controlling, by various form of *yogas*, the material breaths enveloping the lifeforce, thus freeing it from the dense energies which imprison it. All the texts of the *Vedic Scriptures* agree that it is vital for the human being to succeed in coming into contact with this force in the course of his terrestrial life, since the material body in which he will reincarnate will be the fruit of the actions accomplished in this present life. Indeed, in the *Vedic Scriptures*, that the soul, an indestructible lifeforce, changes body is taken as an obvious fact.

Even modern science – which does not believe in the soul's existence but which at the same time cannot explain where the energy that emanates from the heart finds its source – must recognize the continual transformations undergone by the body: its passing from childhood to adolescence, then to maturity and old age. When, at last, the body reaches its final stage, the soul inhabiting it passes to another body; there is physical and psychological change but the individual essence remains unaffected.

The ultimate Vedic message: souls are parts of a Suprasensitive Whole. They can be compared to the countless light molecules in the sun's rays: spiritual sparks, they are the Total Universal Soul's radiance and constitute its transcendental energy.

As part of supreme perfection, the soul is itself perfect. It does not know illness; it comprises eternity, consciousness and happiness. Only the bodies it borrows are subject to birth, sickness, old age and death. If, in one way or another, the individual can relate to the soul, he then sets himself free from identification with the finite physical envelope. He heals from all rebirths, from all illnesses and from all deaths. **HE IS the soul**.

Through the appropriate use of sound and music, we will see that it is possible to get closer to this state and eventually, to reach it.

The soul is a scientific reality

Is this assertion still a vague and falsely "scientific" statement?

In the name of science, the very idea of the soul has often been rejected, and again in the name of science, the idea of the soul has returned to us. With this return through exact and reasoned knowledge, the idea of the soul as viewed scientifically is stronger than ever. Until now comfortably ensconced in his observation of matter, the scientist is suddenly perplexed. Is it that he has gone too far in his explorations? At its finest level, matter (which the scientist blindly believed in) has proved to be... **energy**! And with a single atom stroke, this mysterious energy sends all his hypotheses into the waste-basket.

Something has eluded him. Confronted with an emptiness inconceivable for his sensory powers of observation, he continues to battle desperately against "foundering" in what he calls metaphysics, still the supreme heresy of the materialist, on a par with gnostic physics and **revelation**.

Modern science's malaise is well-deserved since it is responsible for the destruction of the myths which guided the existence of past generations. Through its technological achievements, science harms human beings by offering them the luxury of apparent physical comfort at the cost of inner life. Science could be likened to someone who traps a bird within a guilded cage but fails to feed it. After a time, though the cage continues to sparkle brightly, the bird is dead. Such is the face of modern society, which shines through its technological success but remains in a state of utter confusion at its lack of inner life.

Paradoxically, it is thanks to science itself that this ancient paradigm is being shattered. This state of affairs caused Aurobino to remark: "Perhaps nothing is more remarkable, more suggestive than the way modern science confirms in the realm of **Matter**, the concepts and formulae arrived at, using a very different method, by the *Vedanta*, the ultimate part of the *Vedic Scriptures*. The original *Vedanta*, not that of the school of metaphysical philosophy but of the *Upanishads*." When we examine the question of the soul, the meaning of life, humankind's place in the cosmic process, we no longer get the impression that these questions are considered as non-scientific. These interrogations have often been put aside and rejected in the "hell" of doubt and irrationality. Poets and mystics were heretics for the School, as gnostics were – and, alas, as they still are – heretics for the Church... Aggrandizing for neither the School nor the Church.

The cause of this pitiable (and political) fanaticism was the sad victory of the fragmentary and mechanical thought process over the intuitive and holistic thought process. It was a momentary victory. In a time of obscurantism, the scholar established his set of "initial conditions" – put forward his dogmas and tolerated the idea of the soul as a starting point (since in his calculations, everything was strangely "predetermined"!...). The advent of the quantum image has literally shattered the ancient paradigm of material determinism and has proven the lack of logic in blind faith in local causality.

Unfortunately, the dread of physical emptiness still causes societies to act according to the 19th century's outdated concepts. The desperate fragmentation of social actions prohibits all harmonious cooperation with nature. The idea of finality and interaction of natural phenomena is not "feasible"! Fortunately certain scientific circles are sounding the alarm and refusing to remain confined within the fragility of a purely materialistic concept of existence, a concept which has nothing to do with reality anymore since the advent of quantum physics. By discovering the reality of the Great Quantum Whole, at the same time these new scholars have recognized the interconnection between the whole and each of its parts.

This is exactly the Vedic definition of the nature of the distinct soul, the jiva (the part) in relation to the Supreme Soul, the *paramatma* (The Great Whole)... The tenets of science are about to coincide with those of metaphysics. The scientist has discovered "global" causality and at the same time has deeply disturbed materialistic reductionists who, to some extent, have lived in fear of the return of the unrelenting, millennium-old concept of "finality". Global interaction, the total interrelation of the universe's elements, came to replace matter which henceforth became an infinitely more subtle concept: "energy-matter". Physical reality was no longer the only reality but merely a potential aspect of energy!

Einstein was a unique revolutionary and logically, his conceptual revolution should have lead the humanoïd to a new art of living and new values regarding his daily existence. Were this the case, everything could have or should have changed. But nothing has changed and humanity still worships inert matter, in which it unconsciously sees the image of a genuine lost deity.

We can rightfully ask ourselves why the quantum image has not revolutionized the world. Where does this fear stem from, this contempt for reality?

For thousands of years the *Upanishads* have provided an exemplary definition of quantum physics:

> "The Absolute Truth is a complete Whole and its perfection being total, all that emanates from It, like the phenomenal world, also constitutes a complete totality in itself. All that proceeds from the Whole is a whole in itself and because truth is by nature absolute, It remains the Complete Whole even though countless unities, equally complete themselves, emanate from It." (Iso-Invocation)

Quantum thought views the universal life as a Great Whole where all things are interrelated and constitutionally dynamic. Vedic thought is holographic and views each of life's fragments as a Complete Whole in perpetual movement issuing from the Great Whole. Quantum thought and Vedic thought see the world in a state of eternal interconnection. Reality is movement, energy; nothing is static. Forms are but eventualities, aspects of localized energy, and **one part cannot be modified without influencing another part and without remodeling the whole.**

This is of utmost importance if we are to fathom the profoundest effects sound has on the entire organism. It bears repeating: there is no local causality. The quantum universe is a world of non-separability. In the Vedic view, microcosm reflects macrocosm. Everything is linked, tied together, united, inseparable. A gesture, a word, a sound, a melody, an assertion, a thought, all these act upon **the entire organism and the entire universe**.

By proving the non-separability of all life, of all energy, science has now reached the same conclusions as Vedic revelation. What science calls "matter-energy", Vedic revelation calls *prabha* or "higher energy"... Given the dynamic eternity of this "higher-matter-energy'' (the soul) the existence of the form, the object, or its local configuration (the body) is as fleeting as a dream. A fantastic lifeforce, this atom of higher energy is forever a source of life, of conscience, of serenity, of movement, of eternal freshness and of sovereign power capable of mastering negative emotions and the unfavourable circumstances linked with the existence of physical duality in this world. These negative emotions, fears, worries and deep conflicts result from identification with the ephemeral body and failure to remember the existence of ''the collective self'' as **higher-matter-energy interconnected with and inseparable from the cosmic Great Whole.**

Resuming contact with this reality frees us from the most dreaded of solitudes and cures us of life's everyday deceits. Liberation from these illusions is the sole means of ensuring a perfect and lasting state of health in the human being.

Matter – higher energy – knows neither destruction, nor ignorance, nor pain. It is *Sat-Chit-Ananda*: pure existence, pure conscience and pure happiness. It is perfect harmomy, vital rhythm. When all the fragments of higher energy sing in unison in the light of this consciousness, the cosmos finds a state of supreme balance; it vibrates at the inconceivable speed of a unique high frequency: the music of its soul.

In conclusion, one may rightfully ask whether or not the soul is a scientific reality. On one side stand physicists and doctors (who in fact have come to disagree, since it is difficult for physical realities to break through the sad resistance of scientists who manage the revenue generated by research and the biological medicine of the ''majority''). On the other side stand the poets, visionaries and ''minority'' (or if one prefers, ''complementary'') therapists who warn us that the soul cannot be perfectly understood through laboratory studies...

In the midst of this charming battlefield, the observer, listening to his body, thoughts, hopes, dreams, reasons for living, choices, desires, imagination and ideals, passes quietly by and says: ''This is what I saw and heard; this is what I have lived through. I do not know if it is scientific, political or metaphysical, I only know that it is.''

CHAPTER 1

THE MYSTERIOUS INFLUENCE
OF SOUND VIBRATIONS

"Let us suppose that for days, months, years, we constantly listen to the same melody; over time would not its ever-repeated emotions eventually leave an indelible mark on our personalities and the nature of our emotions?"

Cyril Scott
Music

"The field opened to the musician is not a paltry seven-note scale, but an immeasurable scale, still almost entirely unknown, where only here and there, separated by thick unexplored darkness, a few of the millions of tender, passionate, courageous and serene keys which compose it, each of them as different one from the other as one universe is from another universe, have been discovered by a few great artists who do us the favour of awakening in us the correspondant theme they have found, to show us what wealth, what variety is hidden, unbeknownst to us, by the great inscrutable night of our soul, which we take for emptiness and obscurity."

Proust

A journey on uncharted waters

Antiquity was well familiar with the therapeutic nature of music. It used music to forge moral change, knowing that illness only attacks where it finds weakness and that more often than not, weakness stems from moral impurity. The saying "In purity is strength" remains a basic truth. To be efficient, the composer, like the listener, must develop an art of living which is in harmony with the laws of nature and respectful of the true values of existence. Without such an art of living, one only creates confusion, disharmony and chaos. When the science of sound becomes perfectly known and once it spreads throughout the western world, we will become aware of the countless influences that our subtle and substantial bodies currently endure as we submit them, sometimes voluntarily, sometimes not, to staggering quantities of noises, sounds, rhythms and all kinds of melodies whose effects we know nothing of.

"The composer, in particular," says Cyril Scott, "sets out on a journey on uncharted waters while he awaits inspiration. What he receives can elevate and inspire just as it can have the opposite type of influence. His responsibility is great, although he is often unaware that he bears it."

Furthermore, radio today has taken such a place in our lives that the listener is subjected to any and all sorts of musical material, anywhere, at any given time and under any and all circumstances. There exists a global unconsciousness of the indelible effects of sound on the subtle elements of conscience and memory. Like everything else in the universe, in and of itself radio is neither good nor bad. The way we use it determines the nature of the effects it has on the organism as a whole.

The binding force of harmonic resonance

Reading Cyril Scott's renowned book, *Music, its secret influence through the ages*, is enough to realize that in this area, the greatest of prudence should guide our actions. In his work, re-printed several times since it was first published in 1933, Scott analyzes in detail music's effects on the mind and on the world of emotions. It shows us, for example, to what extent Handel's music influenced the Victorian era, how "his solemn and reverential music awakened in people of certain temperaments a marked feeling of exaggerated seriousness, expressed through a morbid inclination for funereal decors, and how this was the result of a misconception of religion and of spiritual life in general." It also shows us how Beethoven was a psychologist-musician and how his musical style had extremely liberating effects on the subconscious.

Sounds do in fact act as a stimulus which generates a thought process and liberates the energies stored in the subconscious. There is indeed reason for concern when this school of thought is applied in today's world given certain particularly aggressive and openly sinister musical types. Handel's music vibrations influenced his epoch and those of Beethoven's symphonies have an effect on listeners' minds. Likewise, the violently destructive vibrations of certain syncopated rhythms create in those who are fans of these noxious musical styles subconscious reflexes which vibrate through the phenomenom of resonance, attuned to emotions associated with violence and destruction. It is humanity's duty to initiate serious studies focussing on this topic to inform those unfortunate victims who cannot find in this type of music anything but what it proposes: frustration, pain, anxiety and destruction. Each musical vibration binds us to its corresponding level of existence. Through harmonic resonance, we are therefore linked with the entities who inhabit these subtle levels. Some are angelic, others fundamentally demonic. To be aware of this reality enables us to choose consciously the specific association which corresponds to the nature of our desires...

Some musical pieces are harmful, others, on the contrary, have calming and regenerating effects. If some form of music excites, others stimulate without enervating. According to Cyril Scott the orgiastic character of syncopated rhythm deliberately rejects all spiritual and elevating content, producing instead an overstimulation of the nervous system and a weakening of the powers of thought concentration and self-control.

In the light of this information, we can no longer wonder at the frightening number of suicides, depressions, and drop-out behaviours rampant in our world, a world crippled by the mind-destroying rhythm of ''disco'' music and heavy industry.

Ignorance, passion, virtue

Many scientific works have been written on psycho-acoustics and they can be used as a source of reference. Unfortunately, these books are often written in a specialist's jargon. It is not necessary, however, to be an expert in the matter to sense the different effects of sound vibrations on the mind and body. It is enough to close one's eyes, let the determined energy of the music penetrate into our beings and let its effect overwhelm us. Even if the secrets of the theories of therapeutic music, of neurology or of musical semantics are unknown to us, our inner voice, which knows all and understands all (some people refer to it as our common sense...), will dictate three major conclusions depending on the feelings we perceive.

Traces of these three groups of feelings can be found in the best-known Sanskrit text: *The Bhagavad-Gita*. This text, eternally fresh, clearly shows how humans are conditioned by certain forces or modes (*gunas*) inherent to the physical plain. These forces fall into three main categories known respectively as the force of ignorance (*tamas*), the force of passion (*raja*) and the force of virtue (*sattva*). According to the text, all material nature is composed of these three energies. When the living being encounters physical nature, he is systematically conditioned by it. Obviously, a combination of these three modes can influence the individual who is born into this world. At times, a mixture of passion and ignorance will cause him to react in one manner or another; at other times, virtue and passion will cause him to make one gesture or another, to utter one declaration or another. Be this as it may, it would seem that all of matter, including culture and art, is directed by these energies and music is no exception to the rule. A composition, therefore, is always permeated, in one way or another, by nature's three modes and consequently, it influences the listener through the corresponding energy. We will see how it is possible to discern the energies present in all musical vibrations so prevalent in our current communications-oriented system. Whether we are willing or not, whether we are aware or not, they incessantly act upon our patterns of behaviour, our tastes, our attitudes, on our personalities and ultimately, on our destinies. The sensations we can experience while under the influence of a given musical energy are infinite. However, they can be classified according to three principal groups which correspond to the three *gunas*:

1)   The musical energies of ignorance:

Such music makes me feel indolent, insensitive, indifferent, inert. I feel exhausted, completely unenergetic; I become lazy, inactive, lethargic. I sink into a stupor, an uncaring attitude. I lack the will to take action, I lack enthusiasm. I feel pessimistic, negative; nothing is of any importance. I feel that I am harbouring illusions, that I am mentally disturbed. Everything is dark and obscure. The conclusion I can draw is that these musical energies beget within me the energy of ignorance or inertia.

2)   The musical energies of passion:

This type of music arouses in me the thirst of limitless burning desires. I feel growing in my heart the signs of deep attachment, selfish ambitions, uncontrollable desires. It makes me feel greedy. The conclusion I can draw is that these musical energies beget within me emotions linked to the mode of passion.

3)   The musical energies of virtue:

This type of music calms me, relaxes me but does not make me drowsy, soothes me while stimulating me. It makes me more self-confident and helps me concentrate. It elevates my thoughts to beauty, goodness, truth and honesty. It elevates me towards superior realities, towards love, towards God. It enlightens me and brings me a sense of happiness. I feel a stream of purifying light enter me through all the doors of my body. The conclusion I can draw is that these musical energies beget within me virtue.

A transcendental power

At times, the mode of passion dominates and drives away virtue and its influence. At other times, virtue predominates over passion; and at still other times, the *guna* of ignorance triumphs over virtue and passion. In this manner, the three energies constantly compete with one another. The *Vedic Scriptures* show how extensively the three modes of material nature are involved in each of the world's activities. To escape from the spell of the three *gunas* is to free oneself from the limits imposed by the material atmosphere. Thus, the incarnated individual who is able to transcend these forces liberates himself from the yoke of rebirths and deaths and from their relentless anxieties and is able to enjoy exquisite happiness in this very life. In his own interest, the listener who is aware of this reality will strive to listen to music which either cultivates virtue or goes beyond all three modes of energy, completely transcending virtue, passion and ignorance.

In the following chapters, we will see how certain sound energies contained in the vibrations of specific mantras, when they are chanted or listened to, can lead us towards a virtuous art of living marked by peace, health, equilibrium and happiness. We will also see how the sound of Sacred Names contains an energy form (in Sanskrit *param shakti*, superior inner energy) which has the power to thwart the ill effects of the modes of material nature. Music with the transcendental power to go beyond virtue, passion and ignorance can gradually deliver the listener from the chains that keep him within the narrow confines of his physical self. Such music unlocks the door to our inner selves and propels us towards the immeasurable vastness of the soul's life.

A new musical aesthetic

Many people wonder about the effects of music on the living being. Based on the latest accomplishments of musical therapy experts, or by mere intuition, they perceive the urgent need to reorient musical writing. Whether they be practitioners, specialists, musicians, music-lovers or simply listeners, they have concluded that establishing a new musical aesthetic is essential. Psycho-acoustics has been studied and put into practice by many ancient civilizations and is about to resurface for application in the modern world. More and more studies and research projects have been undertaken with a view to better understanding the human reaction to the sound phenomenom. The time for such work has indeed come. In a world where sound pollution is omnipresent and where it is a source of disequilibrium and illness, it is imperative that sound itself be used as a balancing and regenerative element. Today, being a musician is not enough. The creator of music has the responsibility of being aware of how his creativity affects individuals, those who will suffer its consequences, whether good or bad. He is responsible for his music, like a tree is responsible for the fruit it bears. If the fruit of a tree is poisoned, what will the gardener do? If wise, he will cut down the dangerous tree to eventually throw it into the fire. The great wisdom of the cosmos acts in the same way towards societies and empires. When their fruit is no longer healthy, it is eliminated. And what is art in general – and music in particular – if not the most evident fruit of any human civilization, the fruit that best reflects each civilization's desires, inclinations and states of being? Viewed from the perspective that the object of existence is elevating the individual through science, philosophy and art, it becomes obvious that humanity must empower itself to choose a musical form which favours spiritual life and global reharmonization.

Pythagoras' melodic remedies

Music is a balm that soothes the heart. Through the power of suggestion of rhythms and certain melodies, it offers an antidote for human actions and passions. The neo-Platonist theosophist Jamblique states in his writings that Pythagoras deemed it possible for this suggestive power to contribute significantly to good health provided it was used appropriately. The healing processes so begun he termed purification. In this way, he invented remedies that would repress or expulse illnesses from the body as well as from the soul. For his disciples, he developed and adapted what are referred to as apparatus or devices, divinely creating a mixture of certain diatonic, chromatic or enharmonic melodies. Through the latter it was easy to transfer or redirect the soul's passions – sadness, anger, pity, cravings, pride, sloth and vehemence – provided they had taken shape recently or in secret. He righted each passion according to the rules of virtue, tempering them with appropriate melodies which could be likened to beneficial medicines. Each night when his disciples would withdraw to sleep, with certain odes and songs he freed them from diurnal disruptions and turmoil, purifying their intellectual faculties of the fluctuations of their bodily nature and thus ensuring for them a calm night's sleep and pleasant and prophetic dreams. When they awoke, with other songs and appropriate modulations either played on his lyre or sung, he freed them of the sluggishness and torpor brought on by the night. Thus it is possible, according to Pythagoras, to purify the body and the mind using musical energies.

The Su Ma T'sien manuscript

Trust in the transformative power of sounds was also widespread in China, where musical science was a part of the nobility's education. In the very ancient text of Su Ma T'sien's historic memoirs, dating back to the first century B.C., we discover that the right notes act in a beneficial manner on the human's conduct.

> "Sounds and music agitate and animate the arteries and the veins. This generates life-giving breath and brings to the heart harmony and rectitude. The **kong** note affects the spleen and brings saintliness to man. The **kio** note affects the liver and brings the harmony of perfect goodness to man. The **tche** note affects the heart and brings the harmony of perfect rites to man. The **yu** note affects the kidneys and brings the harmony of perfect wisdom to man."

Reading this manuscript makes it clear that in ancient China, healing physical disorders through sound vibration was common. Moreover, the Su Ma T'sien manuscript, quoted by Dane Rudhyar in his very beautiful book *The Magic of Tone and the Art of Music*, demonstrates that the Chinese rightly believed that all musical notes spring from the heart. The ancient manuscript explains that the sentiment, born of inner excitement, manifests itself on the exterior as sound. When the sounds are beautiful, they are what we call musical notes. Hence, (and this is where the written message takes on its fullest meaning), the notes of a troubled period are those of hatred and irritation and its government is one that runs contrary to reason. The musical notes of a country falling into ruin are sad and worry-laden and it weighs down on its people; sounds and notes reflect the government of their time. Analyze the music of a people, of a nation, of a race and you will have a clear image of the motivations, desires and priorities of its individuals. We can confidently say: "Tell me what you listen to and I will tell you who you are".

Preventing the extinction of the heavenly principle

History has taught us that ancient Chinese music left no room for speculation. It was regulated by noble-hearted kings. The leaders of the time were aware of the immense influence of musical vibrations on the people's behaviours. These kings knew that an unregulated way of life leads a society to disaster. Consequently, to a certain extent, ritualistic art, dance, painting, and especially music were regulated, thus establishing moderating principles for humankind. Music could never be violent so that it could not provoke violence. It could not be sad so that it would not draw listeners into a harmful state of mind, it could not center on feelings of anger and fear so as not to encourage anger and fear in the soul.

Humankind is moved by an infinite number of objects. If men's affections and hatreds have no rules, then as man is confronted with objects, he will be transformed to correspond to them. The heavenly principle within him will become extinct and he will be ruled solely by human passions.

In ancient China, music unified the body, the heart and the mind. As it is too often the case today, when anarchy rules how music is used, it did not serve to divide. This dispersion of the physical, emotional and mental bodies leads to serious imbalances which in turn cause fatal sociological pitfalls. Always, new composers have been called upon to create musical forms that unite feelings and produce a calming effect. They help us rediscover our true spiritual identity and prevent the extinction of the heavenly principle in our societies. Music can better the heart. It serves to teach because it has the power to move us profoundly and because it brings change to customs and habits. Consequently, the ancient Chinese kings ensured that music was consistent in measure and number. This is not to say, as some will undoubtedly be quick to claim, that a somber and austere atmosphere prevailed. Music produces joy. But joy manifested in the absence of an art of living brings forth disorder. Sensual pleasure, for instance, when it knows no limits, when it is not controlled by consciousness, can only produce cellular disorders and incurable illness. This is why ancient China established a rule, an art of living, and decreed that sounds be sufficient to create pleasure, but not to the point of laxity. All those who created music did so with the objective of attaining a moderated joy. The goal sought by music composers concerned with the inner workings of humankind and the expansion of its consciousness has always been to counter excesses and soften mores.

Working towards moderation, self-mastery, gentleness and expanded horizons is always better accomplished in simplicity.

Simple music which speaks to the soul

Great music is always simple. If not, if it is too sophisticated, it fails to move us and fails to do its proper work. All that occurs in this case is a type of sterile and disheartening intellectual excitation. In *The Invitation to Music*, Roland Candé has this to say on the subject:

> "The great music of the modern era is much more difficult to play than the music of other eras. The average amateur pianist is unable to play anything composed by Boulez or Stockhausen, nor even the works of Schonberg or Webern. Part of today's music is even so difficult to play that it demands specialized performers. It is not for me to say whether this is good or bad. It is quite an extraordinary fact. Today's music, with its difficulties, cannot hope to be classical tomorrow."

Thus, if we want to provoke an emotional response and feel the transformative effects of musical energies, we should search for a harmonious art of living and a type of music which does not call for intellectual analysis, but on the contrary, which directly touches the deepest recesses of the heart, music which speaks directly to the soul.

Music as a marketing tool?

Most of the time, we do not listen to music, we hear it. Few people have the ability to listen because listening is the gift of one's self to others. We will return to this point at a later stage. But what happens when we hear music? It has an effect on us, beneficial or otherwise, it stimulates us or makes us drowsy. It could be background music which we pay little attention to but which works insidiously on our nervous system as a whole. Let us imagine, for example, walking into a store. Music pours from loudspeakers but we do not really listen to it; we ignore it. We go straight to the department which interests us without a second thought for the music being played around us. But the music is aware of us. It is interested in us. It cunningly penetrates into our bodies through what scientist Thomas Zébério calls vortex-ring interstices, which are in fact the electromagnetic centres of our body. Through these centres, music spreads and fulfills its mission: breaking down our defence mechanisms and encouraging us to buy products we do not really need. Our discernment is paralyzed and we are soon filling our bags with all kinds of unnecessary purchases. Such is the function of music as a marketing tool.

In Rolando Benenzon's book on musical therapy, we find an account of the experience of Italian physiologist Patria, who conducted historical experiments and was able to determine the effect of certain sound combinations on the blood's circulation to the brain. Among other forms of music, he used military marches such as the "Marseillaise" and was able to ascertain that blood circulation in the brain increased when the subject listened to military-type music. Be it used for marketing or military purposes, so to speak, quite obviously music acts upon our cellular system as a whole. As Ralph Tegtmeier remarks in his *Guide to New Musics*:

"We do not generally try to entertain a perfectly conscious relationship with music. It is for us a source of liberation, often perhaps the only liberation we really know, and for this very reason we overestimate it. Once we reach this point, we become incapable of mistrusting it and are unable to protect ourselves effectively from the abusive influence it can have."

A state of vigilance

Another thought process exists: that of remaining constantly aware of the musical energies which surround us, penetrate into our systems, exercise their suggestive powers on us and thus make us subject to their influence. This process is a state of vigilance, a war-faring attitude where the human body and the human heart serve as a battlefield. Here the word heart designates the subtle heart situated a little behind the physical heart. It is in this tiny organic computer that music's emotional and sensory forces are processed. It is often necessary to be extremely vigilant and constantly on one's guard to protect oneself or, on the contrary, to take advantage of the beneficial effects of musical energies and the many types of sounds which saturate our current environment. In his musical therapy manual, Professor Benenzon, a child psychiatrist, asks:

> "With the incredible development of sound in our current civilization, what changes have been brought about in enzyme-based mechanisms? We have no clear idea yet, but in all likelihood, these changes do not bode well for the future."

We are compelled to recognize that the vast majority of sounds produced by the "machine age" – whether described as musical or not – in both the adult and the child result in alarming functional disturbances and these sounds can be unhesitatingly categorized as harmful to the human's well-being and prejudicial to his evolution. But are we conscious of the short-term effects of sounds on our organism? Trustingly, year-round, we absorb all sorts of rhythms, tunes, melodies and harmonies which are repeated *ad infinitum.* Do we realize that the same music replayed over and over again over a period of days and months produces emotions which wear an indelible furrow into our personalities, thus influencing the course of our lives? Before becoming fully aware of music's effects on our soul, let us ask ourselves to what extent sounds influence our physical body!

Cows that love Mozart

In scientific circles, the norm is to collect data from experiments on plants before using animals as subjects. When effects on fauna and flora are evident, experiments are conducted on human subjects. Let us examine this scientific integrity keeping in mind the following finding, as described by Professor Benenzon:

> "An Illinois farmer planted the exact same type of seeds in two greenhouses, under identical fertility, humidity and temperature conditions; in one greenhouse, he placed a speaker which broadcast music twenty-four hours a day. After a while, he noticed that in the building where music was played, the corn crop had sprouted more rapidly, kernels weighed more

and the earth was more fertile; plants closest to the speaker were damaged from the effect of sound vibration. The experiment proved to be so successful that in Canada, music is currently used in several agricultural operations and it has been observed that sound vibrations destroy a micro-organism (parasite) which is harmful to corn crops. In veterinary medicine, it is often laughingly said that cows love Mozart but on the other hand, that Wagner or jazz decreases their milk production. In American research centres, however, the issue is under serious study. Illinois statistics show that the milk production of cows kept in stables close to airports where jets take off and land decreases to zero because of the surrounding noise level.''

We can no longer ignore the powerful effects of every type of sound on life in general. Music affects plants, animals and human beings. It conditions them to behave in certain ways. It "programs" them in one sense or another. The use of melodic and rhythmic sound vibration is an age-old practice, turned to since time immemorial to maintain or transform the level of consciousness and subsequently, to reestablish equilibrium in the body as well as the mind.

Cascading splashes

If you immerse a tuning fork vibrating at exactly 440 cycles per second into a glass of water, you are sure to get wet, since on contact with the water, the tuning fork will produce a cascade of splashes. In laboratories, the tuning fork has long since been replaced by electronic sound generators which have become the instruments of psycho-physics. If the vibrations of a simple tuning fork can produce a cascade of splashes, what is the power held by the vibrations emanating from a symphony orchestra or a rock music recording?

Clearly, all musical sources produce a measurable and quantifiable power which influences and controls us. Whether we like it or not, whether we are conscious of it or not, this vibrating force penetrates us. It introduces itself into our systems and settles in each of our cells and spreads its destructive or creative power, beneficial or harmful. Some forms of music have the power to make us more aggressive; others can bring out our gentler instincts. Just as electricity can produce both cold or heat, music can be the driving force behind peace or war. It is a neutral energy; we are responsible for its ultimate effect. We must shoulder the responsibility of our desires, we must be aware of what we really do want. Do we want to be violent? Then let us listen to music that seems to be violent. Do we want to live in peace? Then let us surround ourselves in soft and peaceful music. The choice is ours: to quench our thirst with heavy and violent vibrations or to find our nourishment in pure waves and high frequencies. Hélène Caya, at the end of her book entitled *Du son jaillit la lumière* (*From Sound Springs Light*) states: ''The gentler music is, the more love it transmits.'' And being gentle in no way precludes being strong.

A matter of free will

True strength is not a momentary state of excitement which consumes the organism's reserves. On the contrary, it is a gentle and irresistible energy, luminous and powerful. On this level, nothing is good and nothing is bad. It is up to each of us to recognize what we want to achieve by listening to a particular musical energy, to develop the sensitivity required to feel its effects on our bodies and our minds. All we need do is listen attentively, to refuse to blindly submit ourselves to the influence of vibrations and to examine our reactions when music's invisible waves reach us. Are we nervous? Are we calm? Do we want to remain in a state of nervous tension? After analysis, a decision is imperative. If we judge that a certain type of musical wave produces harmful effects within us, causing nervous fatigue, lack of concentration or aggression, nothing prevents us from suppressing the source whenever it is possible to do so. Nothing prevents us from turning off the radio or the television or changing stations or channels. Nothing prevents us from leaving a place where music we deem inadequate is being played. It is a matter of free will.

Music and destiny

We rapidly come to realize the following fact: the same compositions, or harmonic and rhythmic arrangements of identical nature, always generate the same emotions and feelings. Here lies the greatest threat and the greatest opportunity. Certain feelings are awakened by music and the experience can be relived several times over. These emotions create habits and the habits in turn shape our personality. An individual's character creates his destiny.

The basic nature of the music we listen to invariably leaves its imprint on our mores, actions and patterns of behaviour. The axiom says: ''Music imitates life and life imitates music.''

Health's No. 1 enemy: noise

According to the most widely accepted medical definition, noise can be defined as a sound which, once it reaches a certain degree of intensity, can lower the body's energy reserves. For some, producing noise is a sign of power. This is why noise has become the scourge of the 20th century. For an industrialized country with a population of approximately 50 million, healthcare costs directly attributable to the effects of noise reach the five-billion dollar level, the same amount of money it takes to fight the harmful effects of smoke addiction... Noise is responsible for 11% of all work accidents and for 15% of all absenteeism.

These figures are probably an underestimate since many sick people cannot properly determine the cause of their illness. Furthermore, many doctors are not yet fully aware of the physical and psychological wounds caused by the shrill of ultrasensitive anti-theft sirens, thunderous jolts of motorcycles equipped with illegal mufflers, the invading rattle of pneumatic drills, the howls of police, fire-fighting and ambulance vehicles and the virtually unbearable levels of over-amplified music. Not to mention the startling and strident sound of ringing telephones and blaring car horns, the sad and horrific banes of our everyday existence, enough to break one's heart.

Noise is the cause of nearly one-quarter of all mental illnesses. By rocking our system until it reaches a state of imbalance, noise subtly attacks our nervous system, unleashing fatigue, dizziness, ulcers, cardio-vascular problems, unhealthy behavioural patterns, hormonal imbalances, depression, if it does not actually lead to sheer madness. Four headaches out of five are caused by noise and they cost society some eight million dollars per day. In very noisy urban areas, the consumption of tranquilizers is far above average. Obsessional, noise often leads to suicide, murder or divorce, as it changes the individual's fundamental personality. There is no physiological tolerance to noise; in other words, the organism undergoes its effects without ever becoming accustomed to it.

The antidote decibel: the song of nature

The antidote against these apocalyptic noises can be found in nature. The music of nature is the easiest road to the abstract garden of immanence and of solar harmony. When we become more sensitive to the beauty of all that murmurs and sings in creation, large expanses open up within us and we feel closer to the Christic intelligence which holds sway over the elements. What results is a harmonization of all the body's cells. This state produces an incomparable sensation which is capable of healing all modifications or injuries noise effects on the organism's structure. A waterfall can make more noise than a combustion engine; but while one exhausts, the other soothes. The rumble of ocean tides is not less deafening than the 90 or 100 decibels of rush-hour traffic, yet it relaxes. Identical decibel levels are found elsewhere as well. Played equally loudly, a heavy-metal rock song seems much more intense than a Mozart concerto, but both produce and emit the same amount of decibels. Let us recall that the decibel (dB) is the scientific unit of measurement for sound; *deci*, for one-tenth and *bel*, for Alexander Graham Bell, inventor of the telephone. A sound ten times louder than another is said to be ten decibels higher and for each tenfold increase in intensity, the sound level increases by ten decibels. A sound one thousand times more intense than another is 30 decibels stronger; a sound one hundred thousand times more intense is 50 decibels stronger, etc.

In their study on sound and hearing, S.S. Stevens and Fred Warnshofsky have written the following on sound waves in an aerial environment (*The World of Sciences*, Time-Life Collection):

> "The decibel provides an approximate relationship between the physical intensity of a sound and the subjective intensity of the sound sensation it produces. To measure the sounds of daily life, a zero-decibel level represents the lowest sound audible to the average ear. Sounds above 130 decibels become physically painful."

When music deafens

Now, let us take a measuring device and go to a rock concert or a disco where sound systems are boosted to the limit. The device easily registers peak levels reaching 120, 130 and even 140 dB! This is beyond the pain threshold and could potentially result in lesions. The "Walkman" is often listened to at high volumes over prolonged periods of time. It causes damage. In France, the Army Review Council has noted progressive deterioration in each successive generation's hearing.

In 1985, Annie Moch, an assistant lecturer at the University of Paris Psychology Department, published an extensively researched study on the subject of hearing loss. Research conducted in the United States indicates that loss of hearing which occurs after a subject is exposed to high noise levels should not normally go beyond 10 dB over a period of two minutes after the exposure, otherwise, permanent deafness will ensue, especially if the traumatism is repeated successively. However, measurements carried out before and after the audition of rock concerts – or recorded music – show a loss of hearing which reaches the 30 dB level among teenagers aged 16 to 18 years.

In a study on music that deafens and noise warfare, Richard Cannavo states that examining the hearing of musicians themselves could provide a good indication of the effects of high noise levels. He writes: "Out of 43 rock professionals examined by scientists, an average loss of hearing of 20 dB was noted after six years of activity". Even classical musicians must be careful. Specialists who examined the 110 musicians of the French-speaking Swiss Orchestra assert that nearly half of them presented hearing impairment and 30% suffered from ringing in the ears and even vertigo.

Acoustic hypertrophy and degeneration

According to the World Health Organization, by the year 2000 the number of hearing-impaired individuals will increase by 20%. This is what makes Richard Cannavo comment: "How very ironic! At a time when music reigns supreme, when it is omnipresent and universal, we see the advent of a generation of deaf children" ! According to a report published by the Leeds' Institute of Technology, almost one million English teenagers suffer from hearing impairment caused by thoughtlessly listening to music at top volumes. We can ascertain that what is conveniently called acoustic hypertrophy is, for the most part, at the origin of a premature aging of the structures of the internal ear. Dr. Claude Illouz, an assistant at the Rothschild Manin Foundation, explains that the level of intensity and the length of the listening period are closely linked to degeneration mechanisms. Sound vibrations of very short duration, if they are extremely intense, are enough to cause an acoustic traumatism. Conversely, a prolonged noise can result in permanent lesions even if it is of relatively low intensity. It is important to note that amplifying systems currently in use often produce noise levels of well beyond 120 dB, particularly in the case of bass notes. Considering the fact that concerts sometimes last a full two hours, it is easy to understand why so many people currently suffer from major hearing trouble.

The problem lies above all in the fact that we remain ignorant of our growing deafness. We can safely say that the residents of huge modern cities suffer from acoustic hypertrophy and all the imbalances it causes at the cellular level. To prevent and cure this destructive and rarely diagnosed illness, it is not chemical tranquillizers that should be prescribed, as traditional medicine so often does. Rather, the new solution should be a regimen of silence, of strolls in nature with birds songs and babbling brooks. For all intents and purposes, I would add that these soft and melodious sounds are particularly effective in soothing the behavioural problems caused by the illnesses of civilization, despite the fact that some critical minds have not yet recognized their true value. Music with the power to relax, as based on serious studies, inspired meditative melodies and all powerful sound vibrations able to heal the troubles linked to exposure to noise should also be prescribed.

In order to perceive the song of atoms or the subtle electromagnetic energy of the life spectrum, today's human beings should stop "making noise". Without this voluntary gesture, man will remain deaf to vibrations of his timeless soul. In "Psychophysiology and Psychophony" (*L'homme sonore*, *The Sonorous Man*, Épi Publishers, Paris, 1977), Marie-Louise Aucher writes:

> "Whoever has seen a little white mouse, submitted even for only a few seconds to a very loud siren, suffer an audiogenic epileptic seizure, lethal in sensitive subjects, will have understood that noise is more than an annoying sensation which we grow accustomed to, more than a source of professional deafness, but the major factor behind nervous imbalance in the modern world. The convulsive effect is accompanied by a general disturbance at the visceral level and by neurotic disorders. The psychophysiologist explains this by localizing the action of the noises in the unifying and regulating centres of the brain stem, centres of the body's wisdom (including the brain of the spirit) which become the centres of the body's madness."

I want to believe that in the near future, new doctors will be more interested in their patients' well-being than in the growth of the barbiturate industry. The music of the soul, contrary to analgesic medication, does not run counter to the Hippocratic oath...

Music influences our feelings

Joseph Stuessy, a music professor at the University of Texas in San Antonio, tells us to be on our guard:

> "All music, whatever it may be, infuences our mood, our feelings, our attitudes and the behaviour they cause."

We find in *The Song of Songs* – a biblical account which is one of the most beautiful love songs ever written – the story of a lovely Sulamite woman and of her love for a young shepherd. Their union is threatened by King Solomon who puts forward all his wisdom and glory to try to conquer the young woman's heart, but in vain. Wishing to remain faithful to her shepherd, the Sulamite woman urges her female companions not to awaken in her the lure for the king who seeks to win her heart. (*Song of Songs, 2.7*). She knows intuitively that the words used to glorify the king can also influence her and alter her feelings. She categorically refuses to listen to them. She does not want to hear them. She recognizes that certain words could have the power to transform her desires and that the behaviour which would result from listening to these words would inevitably conflict with her true feelings.

What should we make of this attitude and the precious teaching it holds in the face of sung music, the major part of the current radio programs which our ears are literally saturated with day and night. Whatever their type, most "commercial" songs are very successful with a large listening audience, often ignorant of the music's long-term effects on its listeners. These songs are broadcast up to ten times a day, creating therefore impression upon impression, influence upon influence and force upon force in the listener's mind. Needless to say, such a bombardment of sound wears a deep furrow in the brain and its inherent desires are directly linked to the sense and to the intention that its authors, composers and performers have chosen, consciously or not, to inject into their creation.

We should not hastily conclude that all sung music is harmful! It cannot be denied that artists sometimes propose texts which inspire one's innermost self and rhythms that elevate and stimulate the body's energies. The cumulative effect of these highly inspired melodies is therefore beneficial. All popular songs which carry authentic feelings, and which are not simply a mindless mechanical repetition with a few superimposed chords, tend to rehabilitate the soul's peace and harmony. However, there is just cause for worry when we consider the violently suggestive words of some "hits". Here again, it is up to each of us to find the right measure of discrimination in evaluating the music we choose to hear. One man's meat is another man's poison... These texts – whether truly sung or bellowed – are nevertheless honest in their intentions. They do not suggest, but directly propose to those who willingly listen to them, the clamour of anxiety and the cries of agony. What devastation these sounds create in the mind!

Fortunately, nothing is permanent and every anomaly can be corrected; "no damnation is eternal". The living being always has the privilege of reform, of redirecting himself towards influences linked to the divine plain, or at least to the virtuous forces of nature. But the harm has been done. Although what is supposedly harmful can eventually become beneficial in the evolutionary sense – since every obstacle is, in reality, a stepping stone – the fact remains that the sociological reactions caused by harmful influences will strongly tend towards violence, base sensuality and depressive nihilism. Hence, the equilibrium or imbalance of societies is the direct result of the music each creates and encourages; and not vice versa. When the musical theme and the sung text produce joy, hope, healthy confidence or else, love without expectations, then there is no contraindication and the mind is favourably influenced.

Rites of passage and the lost meaning of ritual

In a recent conversation Don Campbell, publisher of *The Quest* magazine, founder of the Institute for Music, Health and Education and author of the book *Introduction to the Musical Brain*, talked about rock music as a sound stimulation:

"Having worked with many children with severe intellectual handicaps, I have noticed the use of paradoxical drugs. A child who is hyperactive is often given Ritalin. But anyone who knows the drug well knows that it is "speed", it is not a calming drug, unless the child is already very hyperactive. Therefore, by giving a child the drug – which I do not advocate – physicians succeed in calming him. This is a paradox, and I think the same thing holds true with music. We live in a society in which youth have no rites of passage (a ceremony destined to help the individual surmount a crisis caused by a change in his physiological or social characteristics). My grandfather, and even my father, had no need for the kind of sound stimulation that today's youth need. After school they worked in the field for two hours, they had rhythm within their own bodies, they worked in close contact with nature and were able to regenerate and renew themselves through their own rhythmic pattern. At times, new types of violently rhythmic music (hard rock, hard core, etc.) may seem horribly difficult to bear. They may even be seen as a threat by those of us who do not find in them any aesthetic appeal. But physiologically, we are beginning to see that they may work paradoxically, helping fans to find a support mechanism, a basis, something to hold on to, a way to relieve stress and find a real sense of inner well-being in as much as the current societal system provides no real opportunity for physical exchange similar to the basic spiritual rhythm, as has always been the case in societies outside the West."

Let us therefore recover a sense of ritual, a sense of ceremony, a sense of the sacred and we will no longer feel the need for devastating sonic outbursts. The world's modern thinkers sometimes wonder why society proposes so many forms of entertainment of a perverse and violent nature.

Horror films and pornographic films are countless, as are the premises where the consumption of all types of drugs is tolerated and all these activities are systematically supported by extremely aggressive sound tracks in the background. Don Campbell's remarks hold the answer. For those who are its victims, the total absence of rites of passage in today's society tends to provoke the necessity to compensate for a very basic sociological gap.

Which music provides good listening?

To answer this question, I will not listen to my feelings or my inclinations. Rather, I will knock on a doctor's door. In the last pages of his informative work, *Your Body Doesn't Lie*, Dr. John Diamond shares the fruit of his research – discoveries which corroborate those of numerous other researchers – on music's effects on plants and on the human body. He had the idea of measuring the muscular reaction of patients listening to various types of music.

He reports on his experiments as follows:

> "Using hundreds of subjects, I found that listening to rock music frequently causes all the muscles in the body to go limp. The normal pressure required to control a strong deltoid muscle (a triangular muscle in the shoulder, used to lift the arm) in an adult male is approximately 40 to 45 pounds. When rock music is played, only 10 to 15 pounds of pressure is needed. Every major muscle of the body is linked to an organ. This means that all the organs of our body are affected by a large proportion of the popular music to which we are exposed each day. If we add up the hours of radio play throughout the world, we can see how enormous a problem this is. The abnormal rhythm of rock music's beat (an anapestic rhythm – da-da-Da) and the music's high noise level induces weakness in us. Harmful music decreases physical energy, regardless of the volume at which it is listened to."

Such are the conclusions drawn by Dr. Diamond after years of experiments.

Other clinical research has shown that with an anapestic rhythm, the entire body is plunged into a kind of state of alert. This state provokes a decrease in the attention, span, hyperactivity, anxiety, irritability and constant agitation. It becomes difficult to make decisions and the feeling that things are not going the way they should settles in. Then follows a loss of energy with no apparent cause.

Given such a warning from physicians, one can rightfully wonder if one of the most widely broadcast musics in industrialized countries is not the greatest source of cellular disorders. New illnesses, said to be caused by "civilization", are always caused by pollution. Chemical pollution, psychological pollution and now... sound pollution.

To conclude, we must mention a book written by Hal A. Lingerman, *The Healing Energies of Music*, in which we can read:

> "Destructive music causes damage not only to your physical body, but to your emotions and mental processes. Such sounds affect your entire aura, making you feel psychically torn apart, fragmented, frightened, combative, isolated, tense and aimless. Such stressful, ugly sounds will also scatter

your plans, and they will fog and frustrate your goals. Most tragically, discordant music will alienate you from your inner center of guidance, cutting you off from your conscious union with the Creator, leaving you feeling abandoned, and exposing you to being controlled by negative vibrations."

Calming music

It is urgent that we come to understand to what extent ritualistic, sacred, meditative or devotional music can heal us and provide an effective solution to the disruptive and unbalancing effects suffered by human civilization, to what extent it helps us rediscover the voice of the heart by guiding us towards higher spheres of life, those that we originate from, regardless of our race or religious beliefs. Then, its true role is unveiled and we discover the music of the soul. It provides links that bind one human being to another by providing them with the means to discover their true spiritual identity. Finally, it provides the means of establishing a relationship between the inner self and the Complete Whole, of which the music of the soul is an integral part and whose qualities it shares, beyond any restrictive considerations of time and space.

Be this as it may, it is not easy to be selective in what we listen to today. Music is omnipresent: in the street, in shops, banks, on public transit, at the office, at home, everywhere. We can say that we play an unwilling part in absolute unconstraint. Being one of the most powerful vehicles of social change, music is used anywhere, by anyone, in the most offhand manner! But what is even more alarming is that it is played at higher and higher volumes. Be it in huge concert halls or through the explosive phenomenom of the famous "Walkman", the power of the decibel has been savagely unleashed.

Some physicians have sounded the alarm and fortunately, we are witnessing a counterattack on noise: more and more music lovers are turning to more acoustical, softer, more ethereal music, thereby demonstrating that the song of nature is the most pleasing to the soul.

Professor Mikhaël Aïvanhov says in his lectures:

"Ordinary music awakens human passions. Thus, as soon as it begins to play, we feel pushed to idiocies, we become a little mad. A few young people have admitted as much to me. Upon hearing it, they are ready to embark on any adventure. This music excites them; it drives them quite mad. When will we turn to music that provides a link with the spiritual world, music which calms, appeases and inspires?"

Music that calms, appeases and inspires can soothe the world. No words can be compared to this music. When we are addressed, we are told to be honest, to be kind and to avoid doing to others what we would not like others to do unto us. But these words do not necessarily penetrate the heart. Often, they remain on the surface and consequently, they are ineffective. In this manner, we can not integrate into our lives the concepts they represent. On the other hand, music that calms and appeases produces an image in the thought process and this image, in turn, enters the heart. We come to desire the realization within us and around us, the image of health, beauty, peace, kindness and purity that we have perceived. We make the decision to live what had hitherto only remained on the surface of our own being.

Instrumental music, like meditative song, represents a vibration which offers the advantage of not being expressed with comprehensible words likely to awaken inconsistencies. In the state of mental peace, the spirit of opposition has no opportunity to assert itself. In this way, listening to a sound vibration suggesting physical or moral qualities can facilitate the acquisition of these very qualities.

Hearing and nutrition

Is it possible to modify or improve one's hearing by altering one's nutritional habits? Yes, it would seem so.

Aveline and Michio Kushi, renowned speakers and authors of the book *Macrobiotic Pregnancy and the Care of the Newborn*, mention in their studies that when a newborn's ears are small, pointed at the top and located high on the head, this is a sign of excessive consumption of animal products during pregnancy. The auricle – the visible part of the ear – when insufficiently developed is unable to concentrate and orient sound towards the entrance of the auditory meatus in an adequate manner, appreciably diminishing the intensity of waves on the extremely taut membrane of the eardrum. The importance of the external ear's development is demonstrated in nature by a little desert fox, the fennec, which roams about the Sahara at night. Its large pointed ears catch the faintest sounds its prey produce in the dark.

We see that on the one hand (with the example of the fennec) that the external ear's development constitutes an important factor in the quality of hearing, and on the other hand, (through the research of Mr. and Mrs. Kushi) that proper or improper ear development is determined before birth, by the mother's nutritional habits. Mothers who want their children to have perfect hearing should refrain, at least during pregnancy, from eating any animal food products (meat, fish, eggs), with the exception of dairy products. Those who fear protein deficiency due to the non-consumption of meat should note that their fear is unfounded and that if they wish to enjoy not only good hearing during all their life on earth but also good physical and psychological health, it is strongly recommended to refrain from eating all animal flesh.

In their research on cancer and nutrition, Chantal Drolet and Anne-Marie Sicotte remind us that the 20th century is responsible for radical nutritional changes. An over-consumption of fat, particularly from animals, is undoubtedly the most dangerous of these innovations. In an article on *"Nutritional Habits that Kill"*, published in *Resource Guide* magazine, they state:

> "International studies prove that meat and animal fat are the foods most likely to create a favourable environment for cancer."

Let us recall that one Canadian out of three (an enormous proportion) will contract cancer during his lifetime. In 1988 statistics brought to light 100,000 new cancer cases, including nearly 60,000 deaths. The situation is alarming. Dr. Verner Zabel does not hesitate to write:

> "The human cancer rate is proportional to the quantity of meat man absorbs."

64

Substances morbid to the ear

Is there any relation between cancer, music, good hearing and one's nutritional habits? Yes, indeed!

Music can have an effect, can soothe and can even heal in some instances. However, it remains impotent and ineffective if the listener does not take his own fate into his hands. If he goes on feeding himself in an anarchic way, with no respect for the laws of nature, he will only partially perceive the subtle energies of the rhythm and harmony which can cure him. How can we enjoy good hearing (and especially the gift of clairaudience) when the colon is submerged by the phenomenon of albumin decomposition and when the liver and the body's cells cannot sustain the required level of detoxification?

As early as 1893, Dr. Louis Kuhne in his work entitled *The New Healing Science*, demonstrated the common elements of illnesses and the cogency of a vegetarian regimen. He reasoned that the cause of illnesses was the body's congestion with pathogenic products resulting from poor digestion. Improper digestion is undoubtedly caused, as we can well surmise, by a pernicious and flesh-tainted nutrition. Foreign substances, generated for the most part by the consumption of animal flesh, are gradually deposited in certain areas of the body, particularly in the vicinity of the secretory organs. As time goes by, congestion continues to grow in more remote locations, mainly the top parts of the body, that is to say the neck, the head and of course, the ears...

The process of intoxifying certain cells is impossible and inconceivable without a consequent and intimate relation to other symptoms. When the ears are affected, the entire body suffers from an overload of fermented substances. Poor nutrition leads to poor digestion and in turn, poor digestion provokes an invasion of foreign substances, fermented and gaseous, throughout the entire body. When these substances make their way towards the ears (connected to the trachea by the Eustachian tube), the delicate organ of hearing is obstructed and hardens, fine lesions appear on the eardrum and it can no longer vibrate normally under the action of sound waves. This results in a catarrh of the ear (inflammation of the mucous membrane and hypersecretion of the glands).

Louis Khune explains:

> "Pathogenic products from the consumption of animal flesh are deposited particularly in the centre of the ear. It often happens that acute cases occur and the pressure from below is very strong. Actual purulent abcesses form in the interior of the ear, which must constantly eliminate pus and foreign substances in fermentation, producing the substances which everyone is familiar with. If this acute case is not cured in time and naturally, the consequence is an ever-increasing accumulation of morbid substances and often even the direct destruction of the hearing organ whose condition deterioriates when one attempts to address its acute state with medication."

To better understand what happens in the ear when the body is overloaded, it is necessary to come to understand the importance of the Eustachian tube (named after Eustachi, an anatomist). The tubes equalize the air pressure on both sides of the eardrum, which is sensitive to sound vibrations. This compensation process is automatic and goes undetected as pressure changes are progressive. Abrupt pressure changes during an aircraft landing or when coming down several floors in an elevator, for example, can be felt until one swallows or yawns to open the Eustachian tubes and allow the air pressure to reach proper levels. The Eustachian tubes are incapable of equalizing pressure when an overload of morbid substances obstructs them (in individuals who are suffering from a cold or an infection). The pressure in the middle ear reaches levels below those of exterior pressure because the air in the middle ear is gradually absorbed by surrounding tissue. Uneven pressure on the eardrum dampens hearing and sounds seem to be filtered through cotton wool.

Detecting finer sounds

A vegetarian regimen would make it possible to avoid all these problems. Feeding on fruit, vegetables, milk products and all types of whole cereals liberates the body and mind and enables us to listen to the great universal vibrations, constantly coming towards us, but which we cannot hear because of our obstructed hearing. The music of the spheres and the music of the soul cannot be heard by an ear overloaded with abominable fermentations produced by the digestion of animal carcasses. The agony of the beasts, heartlessly massacred in bloody slaughterhouses, is absorbed by the human body and blocks the superior energies of the divine. Carnivorous humanity becomes powerless to perceive the higher truths of the self and is tragically prevented from gaining access to the influence of miraculous celestial vibrations. "Gastronomic" dishes, ladened with pain, make the human being deaf to the subtle call of the soul's musical energies.

By following a nutritional regimen which is in harmony with the laws of the universe and respectful of the love for life, we open ourselves to the highest sensory perceptions and to higher experiences. We penetrate into the infinite world of virtue. Our eyes no longer see the same colours; our ears detect nature's most subtle sounds. We hear melodies we never dreamed existed. The wind in the clouds, the breeze murmuring among the leaves, the fairy-like rhythm of the fountain become the most wonderful of symphonies. The doors of contemplation and meditation are wide open to us and we discover the incredible music of the inner self.

A meatless regimen facilitates the opening of the "third-ear", the organ of clairaudience. This subtle organ vibrates at a much higher speed than the physical ear and once developed, it provides access to the universe of profound listening, of listening to the self, where we perceive the finest form of music: the music of the soul.

A horrible dissonance

Inner music generates a genuine feeling of plenitude and is the basis of physical and spiritual healing. As long as man goes on ruthlessly killing the living creatures of inferior realms, he will know neither health nor peace and will be unable to perceive the subtle vibrations of the music of his soul. Dr. Paul Carton is adamant on this point:

> "As long as men slaughter animals, they will continue to kill one another. He who sows the seeds of murder and pain cannot expect to harvest love

and joy. The habits of killing and of eating meat are incompatible with the hope of universal happiness and complete wisdom.''

How could any human being hear the song of his soul when his diet, based on meat, draws him closer to inferior species, during sleep immersing his spirit deeply in coarse and inferior fluids? To be aware of the celestial music of the spheres, a genuine panacea for the present afflictions suffered by humanity, it is useful to submit to certain nutritional rules and choosing the foods which make the soul as pure as possible makes our task easier. Vegetarianism is an effective alternative to gain access to purification on the spiritual, animistic and physical levels, a purification that was probably practised by Hermes' disciples in Antiquity.

In *The Hermetic Medicine of Plants* (*La médecine hermétique des plantes*), Jean Mavéric writes:

> "Animal food products are the cause of all organic disorders. Their use is at the origin of the ugliness and the deformities of the races. Cruelty, barbarity and crime stem from carnivorous habits...the true, the beautiful and the good is begotten from vegetarianism."

In certain parts of the world, survival obviously depends on the ability to hunt; when truly necessary, eating meat should not be rejected outright. But at the present time, animals are slaughtered industrially, in an atmosphere of unthinkable terror. As a result, their carcasses are electrified with fear, horror, aggression, anger and revolt. Our contemporaries do not merely absorb meat; unknowingly they feed on all these harmful feelings, along with all that this may imply for the health of their astral and physical bodies!

Many scientists and thinkers have realized the imminent danger for the evolution of humanity that industrial consumption of animal flesh constitutes. Albert Einstein, a physicist of unequalled genius, ardently defended vegetarianism. In his writings on personal development, he states:

> "Vegetarianism, by its purely physical action on human nature, could be a very beneficial influence on humanity's destiny."

One of our leading philosophers, Henry David Thoreau, is of the same opinion:

"I am convinced," he says, "that the destiny of the human race, in its gradual evolution, calls for a stop to the consumption of animal flesh, just as in the same way, wild tribesmen stopped devouring one another once they came into contact with more civilized beings."

The horrible discordance of slaughterhouses gives rise to an uninterrupted series of false notes in the great evolutionary music of humankind. The beast's desperate eagerness and covetous desires are transmitted to men who choose to eat meat. However, a vegetarian benefits from the freshness and stability of plants.

To end this examination of the link between hearing, evolution and nutrition, I would like to once again quote Dr. Paul Carton, who has extensively studied Pythagoras' theories on music and on life in general:

"The Pythagorian diet is a powerful factor in higher human evolution because it ensures the most perfect and harmonious performance of the spiritual, vital and physical lifeforces. First of all, it purifies the mind by sparing it from incitements towards brutality and sensuality. It fosters better intellectual development because it undoubtedly facilitates proper brain functioning. All individuals who abandon the use of meat are amazed to see how their minds become more lucid, their clairvoyant abilities greater and their objectives, loftier. Gentleness, optimism, composure and the sheer joy of living increase progressively. The individual feels transported into a superior world because he has liberated his brain from unhealthy influences, strengthened his moral sense, widened the horizons of his thoughts, facilitated the education of his willpower and increased his spiritual value."

The purifying power of love

As we have seen, virtuous nutrition can facilitate clear hearing. The Vedic text of the *Bhagavad-Gita* goes even further, stipulating that a spiritual nutrition has the power to purify the sensory organs, to produce finer cerebral tissues and to clarify thoughts. Chapter 9, Verse 26 goes beyond simple vegetarianism and lays claim to the purifying power of love:

"If, with love and devotion, I am offered a leaf, a flower, a fruit or some water, I will accept it."

Here, the ultimate devotional aspect of the God-force, the mystical poet of the *Gita* himself, reveals the simple nature of sanctified food. Vegetables, cereals, fruit, milk and water compose appropriate nutrition for human beings and to ''imprint'' upon them higher thought-forms makes it possible for us to progress towards the goal of existence, finally hearing the inner music which will free us from material trappings. Beyond this universal principle, each mouthful tends to bring us deeper into the complexities of our physical nature and the great symphonies of the spiritual realm remain, for us, inaccessible.

According to the *Vedic Scriptures*, the simple sanctification of food through the thought process opens the doors to inner sound. Above all, the esoterical offering should be made lovingly. Indeed, the infinite energy which penetrates all things has no need whatsoever for food! The main factor, the principal ingredient in the preparation of such a magical gesture, is the thirst for absolute love. The solar way is a road which one follows within, in the secret recesses of the soul... The body is a temple. Let us respect it and it will vibrate with the absolute. It will sing in unison with the beauty of the infinite.

Music and digestion

In his book *The Doctor Prescribes Music*, Professor Edward Podolsky, a physicist, considers the value of listening to music during meals. In his opinion, beautiful music played during a meal is of great help in facilitating the digestive process. In his work he describes a scientific discovery which claims that the principal nerve of the eardrum (middle ear) ends at the centre of the tongue and is linked to the brain, reacting to both taste and sound impulses. Commenting on this scientific report, Hal A. Lingerman in *The Healing Energies of Music*, states that it is no longer possible to ignore the close relationship which exists between healthy food and appropriate music. It is not by pure chance that in ancient cultures, expert musicians were invited to play soft and pleasant melodies during meals and feasts.

Let us recall that when unpleasant emotions are felt, the pylorus (a muscular structure situated at the base of the stomach) closes. The stomach's contents can no longer reach the bowel. There follows a bloated sensation, a heaviness, and digestive acids stop working. The result is drowsiness and irritability.

Professor Podolsky writes on this topic:

> "Music is the best antidote for unpleasantness at the dinner table. When there is music to be heard, there is an outpouring of gastric juices. They act as a flushing device. Food is properly digested and it passes from the stomach into the duodenum through a wide-open pylorus."

During meals, music should be simple, joyful, with neither great contrasts nor any intellectual or emotional complexities. Hal A. Lingerman particularly recommends the flute and the harp.

Personally, I have observed that the music said to be of the "Versailles School", which includes the works of Lully, Couperin and Delalande (Symphonies for the King's dinners), creates a climate of peace, joy and opulence which is altogether appropriate to accompany the sacred act of nourishment.

In the *Vedic Scriptures* it is said: *Sevon mukhe hi jihvàdau*; when one uses the tongue to accelerate one's own vibrational rate, the other senses, along with the mental, can be sublimated. Through the nature of nutrition and through the attitude with which we feed ourselves, we can either open or close the crystalline doors of the music of the soul.

Protecting the auditory nerve

The ear comprises three parts: the outer ear (auricle and auditory duct) collects sounds from the environment, they then propagate in the middle ear through the eardrum (a membrane) and the three tiny bones which are joined to one another. Vibrations next reach the inner ear, the cochlea, which sends a message to the brain through the auditory nerve. Such are the constituent parts of this extraordinary acoustic device. The deterioration of one of these parts results in hearing impairment. The lasting sensation of deafness and whistling in the ears one feels when leaving a concert hall or a disco are signs of cellular disorders of the auditory system.

If we wish to perceive the subtle energies carried by sound, words and music, and if we want to do so profoundly and for a long time, so that we may have the privilege of penetrating into the sphere of profound listening, we must protect our ear at all times. There are sunglasses to protect the eyes from too-bright light. Unfortunately, no such thing exists to protect the ear. It is up to us to develop enough awareness to avoid violent noise. Frequent exposure to noise levels beyond 90 dB causes irreversible cellular lesions which on the anatomical level, results in micro-haemorrhaging in the cochlea and on the symptomatic level, in a definitive loss of hearing. Dr. Illouz goes further:

> "From 120 dB and beyond (a normal rock concert) the sound blast has the same effect as a deflagration. It is not rare for the eardrum membrane to tear like the skin of a drum being pounded too violently. Total deafness immediately ensues, accompanied by acoustical phenomena, such as a continuous whistling and ringing in the ears which persists for several weeks before decreasing and then disappearing, sometimes only partially. The inner ear conceals 28,000 vibratory filaments – and not one more. These highly refined cells are miniature, extremely sophisticated computers. Each has its own particular function, selecting information, analyzing sounds, breaking down frequencies before sending through the auditory nerve, an extremely reliable electro-acoustical program, easily decoded by the brain. When one listens intently, the vibrating filaments sway in all directions, sending a message lacking in sound detail. When this happens, we tend to turn up the volume, assuming that we will then be able to hear better. But the more powerful and sharp the sound, the more it is likely to damage the filaments which, unfortunately, do not have the power to regenerate themselves. Obviously, the fewer filaments there are, the less efficient the ear. This is a real vicious circle."

But let us not blame music for every ill. Its harmful effects are simply heaped upon the din of daily living. We should be careful of protecting our auditory nerve if we wish to enjoy concentration, equilibrium, vigilance and attention. Moreover, lesions in the inner ear, once diagnosed, are permanent and irreversible. Blood no longer flows to the parts of the cochlea where necrosis is present: this is cellular death. Hearing aids are designed for the middle ear only (to lessen the effect of lesions to the eardrum and / or the small bones in the middle ear) and because they amplify sounds, they only increase damage levels. We should be forewarned.

Jean-Marie Leduc – in an article on deaf singers published in the February 1989 issue of *Words and Music* (*Paroles et Musique*) – points out that some musicians and hard rock singers exposed to extreme noise levels resort to having wax poured into their ears before they go on stage! But, he goes on to say:

> "While the ears may be protected, nothing prevents sound from exploding in the chest and the abdomen. And as recent statistics from Great Britain have shown, the Number 2 cause of death among international rock stars (after traffic accidents but before drug abuse) remains heart attacks."

When noise becomes too loud, we should immediately think: "Beware, fragile ears". The ear is the organ of equilibrium. Beyond 90 dB, vertigo, memory troubles and sometimes depression can occur.

The importance of knowing what we are exposed to

In reality, the volume of sound should be regulated at all times. American doctors recommend from one and a half to two hours of silence after two hours of listening to a Walkman (at 90 to 100 dB). When subjects are so totally immersed in sound, loss of vigilance, loss of balance and nausea have been detected. Furthermore, it would seem that the ability to perceive physical parameters, for example accurately estimating distance or depth, may be altered.

What could then be said of the miniscule ears of the foetus? Researchers were astonished to discover the extent to which exterior noises reach the unborn child. By placing an intra-uterin microphone close to a child's head, doctors have been able to clearly hear a whole range of noises. Similarly, in Ireland a psychologist has noticed that newborns seem to recognize the musical theme of a television program that their mothers regularly watched during pregnancy.

According to the magazine *Woman's World*, these discoveries could lead to new research aimed at exploring the effects of sound on the foetus' ears. Among other researchers, Conrad Lorentz has established that shortly before birth, sounds are heard and interpreted by living beings. His experiences with birds led him to talk to ducks' eggs on a regular basis. After they hatched, he noticed that the ducklings would come towards him whenever he spoke, as if they already knew him well. The results of this particular experiment were confirmed by other scientists working with chicks, and even with human foetuses, who grew accustomed to their fathers' voices during the gestation period.

How many unknown factors are involved in the way we are subjected to noise and inflict it on others? Researchers across the world should combine their research efforts to determine what kind of traumatism our noisy civilization can provoke in children before they even see the light of day.

A 5,000-year-old message

We find in the authentic comment of the *Vedanta Sutra* (*vedanta*: conclusion; *sutra*: unifying thread) – the *Srimad Bhagavatam* (or *Bhagavat – Purana*), written by Srila Vyasadeva some 5,000 years ago – several accounts which demonstrate how the foetus is capable of hearing exterior sounds. Vyasadeva's very own son – Srila Sukadeva Goswami – had been instructed in the science of bhakti-yoga by his father while still in gestation in his mother's womb.

According to the *Brahma-vaivarta Purana*, Sri Sukadeva Goswami was a soul freed from various material concerns while he was still in gestation. His father, Vyasadeva, sensing that his son would not remain in his company after birth, saw to it that the child, although still in his mother's womb, would hear the message that he had to transmit to instruct him on the principles of inner life.

In the *Bhagavatam*, a vast historical fresco, another account also shows to what extent the foetus is able to perceive words spoken in the pregnant mother's presence: such is the case of Prahlad. The child Prahlad had been conceived by a father of gloomy temperament.

While his mother was residing at the monastery of the sage-musician Narada Muni, the latter spoke at length of devotional philosophy. According to the text, Prahlad had not only heard the great musician's comments, he grasped them. A few years later, he was able to repeat the message he had heard before birth to his classmates, greatly angering his father.

These two references to writings which date back several thousands of years prove that humankind has always been aware of the effects of song and words on the living being, particularly on the foetus. It is worthy of note that Sanskrit verses are poetical texts of great beauty, with elaborate rhythms and metrics. For the most part, they are still sung. When we have the opportunity to read or hear these verses, we can easily understand the vibrations of joy and peace that these children could feel, even as embryos.

The foetus-embryo listens and...understands

In scientific circles, it has become more and more evident that sound waves affect the foetus. Drs. L. Bence and M. Méreaux, eloquent defenders of the premise that music acts upon all living beings, are abundantly clear on this subject. They write in *A Practical Guide of Musical Therapy*:

"During gestation, the foetus perceives a great number of vibrations: heartbeats, the mother's respiration, movements of the abdominal walls, intestinal noises, etc... As early as the sixth month of embryonic life, the foetus' hearing functions and it discerns sounds, especially its mother's voice. Several experiments prove that the foetus also hears music. It memorizes what it hears, thus creating a type of "prenatal sound envelope", according to Édith Lecours' description. Experts speak of a mnemonic encoding which occurs during gestation. This encoding, or memory, is contemporaneous with life in a fostering environment and with the pleasant sensation of weightlessness. This explains why newborns stop crying when they are exposed to recorded heartbeats. This technique is currently used in some nurseries."

Further, Bence and Méreaux write:

> "Through conclusive experiments Professor Tomatis has demonstrated that, as early as birth, babies specifically recognize their mother's voice. This discovery led him to design an *"electronic ear"*, which he uses in the treatment of psychotic children. The device helps children artificially return to the reassuring environment of the womb, filtering their mother's voice and making it sound as it did to the foetus still in the uterus. The baby has two basic needs: its mother's milk and her voice. Later on, music dominates and remains evocative of the mother."

Life is listening

Professor Tomatis, an ear, nose and throat specialist at the Paris School of Medicine, goes even further in his findings. After 25 years of research and experimentation, through rigorous scientific studies he has concluded **that hearing precedes all forms of cellular organization, as if the whole creative process depended on it.** This idea – revolutionary in the eyes of modern science – merely confirms what the Vedic texts put forward several thousands years ago. Tomatis has shown how quick the foetus-embryo is to develop the ear. Why? Simply because life is listening. For him,

> "communicating consists not only in using a given language to address a fellow being, first and foremost, it is opening one's heart to him."

His experiments have proven to what extent the act of listening is ontogenetically rooted in every human being's deepest self. The mother should be fully aware of this fact if she is to help the soul she carries develop the desire to listen, to live, to be free and to love. For listening, it should be recalled, is primarily opening one's heart or, according to Tomatis, "entering into understanding and loving communion with another being". Hence, listening alone is capable of inducing by its presence, communication in the broadest and noblest sense. For, as the founder of the science of audio-psychophonology has said:

"To be a female, is to bear an offspring; to be a woman, is to bear a child; but to be a real mother, is to bear a living being."

The praises sung by the atoms of existence

The mother should speak to the eternal entity who comes from elsewhere, the entity who lives a thousand lives, who has a thousand faces, a thousand parents. It is with this entity that she should converse, and not with a mere parcel of cellular tissues, as some would still have us believe. She will find the words of sufficient strength, the songs of love, the creative and assertive words which will cause the immortal soul – which has found shelter in her womb and whom she already calls her child – to vibrate. From inside herself, the knowing mother hears the praises sung by the atoms of existence and responds to them with the silent song of love. The entity she bears within her is the rhythm, she is the time. In this unmasked state, life is revealed to her through hearing and what she perceives is not the interaction of chemical substances. How could one love a mixture of chemical products, though they may be intelligent? What she perceives of life is this "certain something" which cannot be destroyed, which permeates the entire body, which is immeasurable, which knows neither life nor death and which will never cease to exist. Unborn, immortal, primordial, eternal, this "certain something" has no beginning and will have no end.

This "thing" which, according to the *Vedic Scriptures*, could not be cleaved apart by any weapon, burnt by any fire, dried by any wind, drowned in any ocean, is present as an embryo-foetus is attentive to its mother's love and of all humankind, the unconditional love which is humankind's one and only music; other music being, after all, but a hollow and inconsequential cacophony of sounds. It is this "certain something" that the Psalms of the Bible praise and which speaks to the Provider of life in these terms:

"Thine eyes did see my substance, yet being unperfect; and in thy book all my members were written, which in continuance were fashioned, when as yet there was none of them." (Psalm 139)

The soul-to-soul dialogue

The scientist, with proof in hand, always arrives a little too late. By the time laboratory results have been recorded the life-giving process is already well underway. Fortunately, divine life has no need to be proven in laboratory experiments before it can manifest itself in the hearts of men who seek it. From the dawn of time, mothers have known that the foetus has the ability of perception. This has been proven scientifically. Fine! But how laughable these results are in the face of life itself. As Professor Tomatis remarks:

> "What any mother is able to teach us – that her child moves in the womb when it perceives music, a sound, or a voice – is viewed as a genuine revelation in certain scientific quarters."

Now, we are asked to throw aside this misconception and to begin to understand that not only does the foetus hear, it listens. It listens, understands, and grasps. This truth, demonstrated by Vedic as well as modern science, still has far to go before being accepted by some. We must learn to wait. But the advent of a new cycle in the conscious brings with it an immediate and intimate understanding of what it is to listen. And this heightened sense of awareness is about to wreak havoc among all our old intellectual structures. By developing this consciousness, we embrace life; we understand that in each sound that reaches us is a message from the essential being. To listen profoundly, there is no need for an outer ear. It is but the heart's perception of the invisible world, the soul-to soul-dialogue. This sublime communication is revealed in the Soufi tradition of Master Qusharî.

In his short treatise on the *sana* (esoterical hearing), he writes:

> "Spiritual hearing is the understanding of hidden things by listening to hearts, by discerning realities which are the object of our quest and which comprise the signs of the divine present in all creatures."

The new children

In conclusion, how should the mother communicate with the entity whose body – the basic tool of existence – is developing in and through her? And what should the human being do to enter into dialogue with his brothers and with the Unifying Principle at the centre of his being? One must realize that the words of everyday language are absolutely devoid of meaning to the soul, for it perceives all that goes beyond words. It is the intentionally generated energy, the affectionate warmth carried through a pleasant, soft, loving and compassionate voice that the soul feels. Like the legendary swan which can draw milk from water, the living being draws love from sound. Beyond the foetus-embryo and beyond the dialogue of humans is the Sublime Centre which transcends all science, which is capable of hearing the music of our souls, in spite of the endless commotion of our meaningless thoughts and the disconcerting shallowness of our words. Before the beginning was listening, declares Tomatis, adding:

"Human vitality is based solely on the function of listening."

Now the goal of this auditory contemplation consists in obeying life as it manifests itself genetically. Knowing how to obey the rules of life gives us the hope of one day escaping the laws set by humankind, the non-absolute laws which lead us blindly from bad to worse, towards a risky, dangerous and uncertain future, as long as they remain separate from universal laws. Listening to life will enable us to perceive universal principles: compassion, purity, truthfulness, sobriety; it will lead the New Earth toward the age of mastery. For the mastery of the art of profound listening will be the greatest accomplishment of human evolution. It will provide the pure ambrosia of genuine riches, riches which confer on human beings a state of divine freedom, autonomy and total self-satisfaction. The absence of needs will be an inexhaustible source of humankind's new-found happiness.

New parents, aware of the paramount importance of noise, sound, song and words in their child's development during gestation, will give birth to a new generation, much more advanced than the generation which created the painful industrial world. Nourished with loving and beautiful sound vibrations from earliest conception and throughout pregnancy, these new children will become the architects of a new golden age on Earth.

CHAPTER 2

THE POWER OF SONG AND WORDS

"Let us suppose that a person has absolutely no idea what a revolver is. I put one in his hands saying: be careful, don't press on this piece of metal (I point to the trigger), otherwise an explosion will occur and it could be fatal for yourself or for one of your neighbours. Whether the person believes me or not is of little importance: If he presses on the trigger, the blast occurs. Autosuggestion acts in the same manner... The same holds true for the spoken word which, through repetition, succeeds in automatically penetrating your unconscious."

Emile Coué
Complete Works (Oeuvres complètes)

"The day science begins to show an interest in non-physical phenomena, it will advance more in a single decade than it has in all the centuries of its existence."

Nikola Tesla, Physicist

In the beginning was song

In principium erat verbum: this sentence can be read in the first line of the first paragraph of the Gospel according to Saint John. Various exegetes have given it various meanings, but in general the sentence is translated as: "In the beginning was the Word". In fact, some translators are of the opinion that verbum could mean "sound or song". Be this as it may, sound, song, words or speech are brought forth from the same energy. If in the beginning was the word, or the sound and if the sound was the Divine Principle – as the Gospel states – then its inherent energy must be all-powerful because it is the primeval creative energy. In this sense, the Biblical Scriptures echo the Vedic Scriptures, the latter stating: "In the beginning was Brahman (impersonal aspect of the absolute) with whom was the word, and – the word is Brahman –."

Although religions are often divided because of puerile terminology disagreements, we can find in these two statements a perfect similarity between Hinduism and Christianity. This word, this primeval cosmic sound, can be found everywhere, from the Hebrews to the Tibetans, from Islam to Buddhism. The God-sound is omnipresent in humanity's history and is always closely linked to the essence of the conscious. It is found in the Kabbala and in all great cultures. *Om, aum, amn, ameen, omon, omen, yahuvah*: the list is endless. It is the Logos, the famous lost word of esoterical traditions.

Krishna says in the *Mahabharata*: "I am the sound of ether." Saint John goes as far as mentioning the creative power of the Word:

"In the beginning was the Word and the Word was with God, and the Word was God. The same was in the beginning with God. All things were made by him; and without him was not any thing made that was made. In him was life; and the life was the light of men. And the light shineth in darkness; and the darkness comprehended it not.'' (*The Gospel according to Saint John, Chapter 1, 1-5*)

According to the original Aramean text, ''in the beginning'' implies an eternal state prior to all creation. ''Word'' is simply a transcription of the Latin translation *''verbum''*, of the original *''logos''*, that is to say, the word. This term was commonly used in Greek philosophy to designate the divine intelligence, organizer of the world. According to Emile Osty, a renowned linguistic expert, Saint John gives it the meaning of the substantial and eternal word.

Living assertions

''And the word, we should recognize, is a living entity'' said Victor Hugo. The word is alive; it is a gift from the powers Beyond. When we say ''I am'', we call upon a divine power and gradually, the qualities of our assertions tend to manifest themselves within us. It is quite obvious that the pumpkin does not change into a coach overnight, but the assertion sets in motion the process through which the word takes form in matter. After several repetitions of the sentence: ''I am in good health'', one will tend to feel a sensation of genuine well-being throughout the organism. Try the experiment yourself! In turn, this sensation or emotion will set in motion the phenomenon of health. It is astonishing to observe and realize that this process is effective whether the assertions are made in a state of awareness or not. Furthermore, it is extremely urgent to understand that generally, we use the tremendous power of words in a totally unconscious and negative sense, which is undoubtedly one of humankind's worst tragedies.

The Creator has given humans an unlimited power, that of the spoken word. Yet this power is neutral; it can have opposite effects. The word can constitute the source of our happiness or of our misery. Over a one-week period, should we repeat the assertion ''I am seriously ill'' – especially before going to sleep – in all likelihood our body will weaken and a serious ilness will develop. Should a sick person repeat each day "I am perfectly healed", he will heal if he can conceive of a perfect state of health within himself.

All is vibration

For a long time, we believed that man's primary faculty was the will. Through his research and thousands of healings, Emile Coué proved that it is not the will which is the primary human faculty, but the imagination. The imagination has a direct effect on the organism and this faculty is independent from and stronger than the will. "Imagine" that you are relaxed and your muscles will immediately slacken, your nervous tension will abate. "Will" yourself to be relaxed and you will become increasingly tense. The word acts directly on the imagination. When the human being becomes aware of the power within him, he regains mastery of his life and becomes worthy of his celestial origins. This power could be called autosuggestion, suggestion, the power of the subconscious, etc. What we call it is of little importance. This power has always existed and will always exist. As the holders of this force, we have the right and the duty to develop it and to use it in a beneficial sense.

All this can be explained in a very simple manner, by borrowing data from the field of microvibratory physics. According to Hermes' Law, nothing is inert; all vibrates, all is vibration. For example, if object A vibrates at a frequency of 4,000 cycles per second and object B vibrates at a frequency of 10,000 cycles per second, then objects A and B are not vibrating in harmony. They are not "harmonious", not attuned to the same frequency. To harmonize them, that is to say to put them in tune with each other, it is necessary to make them vibrate at the same speed. Similarly, two persons who do not have similar desires, or who have not reached similar intellectual or intuitive conclusions, will not vibrate at the same frequency and will therefore be antipathetic to one another. When the human being thinks or uses his power of imagination and assertion, he begins to vibrate at the same frequency as the frequency he visualizes. This is simply the phenomenom of vibratory responsiveness.

The invisible bridges of harmonic resonance

What is absolutely extraordinary is to realize that by naming an object with a spoken word, we become perfectly attuned to that object's frequency and we literally enter into contact with it. Everyone knows that the field of action of sound is vibratory. Through the simple action of naming an object and thinking and concentrating on it, imagining all its details, shapes, colours, qualities, attributes which are peculiar to it, the brain projects an impulse towards it. The sound vibration which designates it represents its "counterpart". Therefore, words and names are "supports" or "witnesses" between creative imagination and the object itself. For instance, when the imagination – through the intermediary of the mental computer which is the brain – seeks to attune itself to the **harmony** frequency, the word becomes the vibratory relay between the brain and the state of perfect harmony. In other words, this sound becomes the connection between the archetype and the human being. It makes possible direct contact with the unlimited energies of cosmic harmony, which have existed throughout eternity **within ourselves** and allow us to feel its vibrations. Thus, the word's frequency, the number of sound vibrations it is composed of, builds a bridge, no less real because it is invisible, between us and any given major current of cosmic energy.

At this level, it is not necessary to reason in order to understand but rather to experiment so as to feel and realize. Jean-Jacques Rousseau – one of the Enlightenment's greatest philosopher – had a deep understanding of this basic point when he wrote:

"When man starts to reason, he ceases to feel."

A two-edged weapon

The waves of universal harmony can be picked up if careful attention is brought to this investigation. These waves then permeate the living being's subtle molecular structure and modify the organism entirely. Spoken words, words and names are linked to archetypal objects through their unifying sound. The latter is nothing other than the name by which an object, a form of energy, an element or a person is designated. The great archetypal vibrations are always available in the cosmos, and it is sufficient to attune ourselves to their respective currents to reap their benefits. This "alliance" is forged with the help of both the spoken word and the imagination. Thus, the fundamental frequencies of health, beauty, strength, knowledge, richness, etc., exist in the universe and are constantly available to those who wish to benefit from their vibrations. However, the vibrations of anger, fear, anxiety, poverty and cupidity are also available.

The spoken word is a two-edged weapon. It is for human beings to develop some discrimination in order to have the opportunity to choose, in full knowledge of the facts, the particular energy they wish to tap. The old saying: "Turn your tongue seven times before speaking" wasn't so wrong after all...

The taste for real happiness

Attempting to solve a problem related to exterior circumstances without using the strength of thoughts is a vain endeavour. Only he who takes the spiritual as a basis can experience a sure and solid success. Material planning can undoubtedly provide immediate benefits and occasionally, this apparent profit may even take the form of an overwhelming manifestation. But, according to the laws of life, what is acquired from the exterior does not last. The only lasting success stems from inner activity, from the realm of the spirit. Within us lies the root of all sound images projected on the giant screen of our own existence. A peaceful soul does not seek situations of conflict. The harmony it spreads around itself constitutes the most effective type of protection against encounters with elements or feelings contrary to its ideals or in opposition to the eurhythmy that it continually creates by skilfully conducting the great orchestra of its thoughts. Once the earth is inhabited by such souls, conflicts of interest and great international passions will completely disappear from the face of the planet since they will no longer be nourished by the cacophony, dissonance and disharmony of thoughts. Nations will no longer disagree since they will vibrate in unison to a common note: the taste for real happiness. This superior taste, the genuine music of the soul, will be characteristic of the Aquarian Age into which we have just entered. The taste for the vain sacrifice which marked the preceding age – the sacrifice of man's spirituality in exchange for industrialization – has already weakened and will have disappeared within a few years. If this sacrifice was necessary to build the foundations of the Aquarian Age, it is no longer the case.

The spell-like song of our daily speech

Today, it has become crucial and urgent to realize that this age, expected for millenia, will not manifest itself without the practice of the mastery of thoughts. In a way, thoughts are the reflexes of the subconscious and the only manner in which to actively program the latter is to be "conscious of the conscious", to register or store consciously precise thoughts on the "electromagnetic fields" (or mnemonic engrams) of the subconscious. To do so, we have at our disposal a precious, extraordinary and magic tool, a genuine gift from heaven: the spell-like song of our daily speech, our spoken words. All those who accomplish great things, all those who achieve true success, put their mental and verbal activities in the service of their ideals. How is this done? By recording in the mental process a thought which is precise, persevering, sustained and continuously nourished by the dynamic life-giving force of assertive words. This is in keeping with yoga techniques aimed at mental mastery and in which the repetition of certain series of sounds, all related to the control of breathing, are crucial.

Since Antiquity, the efficiency of these methods need not be demonstrated. In a sense, our daily conversations are a chant and this "spoken word" – particularly when it takes the form of an assertion – acts upon the conscious. In turn, the latter influences the subconscious which, through programmed reflexes, produces the thought. The thought itself is the creator of destiny.

This burning aspect of reality prompted the great master Saint-Germain to write:

> "You allow what you think and what you feel to take on a physical form. You are where your thoughts and words are. You are your consciousness; you become that on which you medidate. Such is the eternal law of life."

At one extreme is the word produced by, and held within, the thought, at the other is destiny. In this sense, we can understand how the word represents the divine power par excellence and the human being, its heir, a potential god.

The living being's absolute divinity

"In the beginning was the Word and the Word was God says Saint John. I am not saying that man is God, as is the habit in popular esoterical circles. At the risk of creating displeasure, I maintain that the universal Soul and the distinct soul never lose their spiritual and absolute individuality.

The study of the oldest book in creation – *The Brahma Samhita* – said to have been written by Brahma himself, has much to say on this topic. It is possible to blend into the energetic impersonal Brahman light, but this pseudo-annihilation proves to be yet another illusion. According to these writings, true liberation lies in the love relationship which develops infinitely in all senses of the word, between the infinitesimal, unique and immutable essence and the Infinite Essence, or Divine Presence, this hero of Love, with a thousand names and a thousand faces, which has always awaited us. An entire range of limitless relationships (*rasas*) can arise from this loving and mystical exchange. The masters of universal devotion have identified five great *rasas* families (neutral, respectful, friendly, parental and conjugal). We cannot further elaborate on this topic without moving beyond the limits of this work. Readers wishing to learn more should refer to the books which deal with the subject of divine love – in particular – *The Imitation of Jesus Christ* (author unknown) and *The Nectar of Devotion* by Rupa Goswami (translated by Bhaktivedanta Swami, B.B.T. Publishers).

If the living being is God, but has ''forgotten'' he is, as some like to claim, then which God are we referring to? How can God, who is omniscient by definition, forget anything? Mere common sense leads us to reject this inconsistency. The living being is not God. However, he is of divine essence and participates in the absolute; he has its qualities, its attributes and its powers, but in infinitesimal quantity. Which, on the human scale, is phenomenal when we imagine the incommensurate powers of the Absolute Principle.

Man is of divine nature. We hold within our souls and on our lips the sound keys of our own destiny and that of the world. Through our assertions, we have the power to create the universe we desire. Coming from a ''Heavenly Father'', what could be more liberal... Émile Dormoy, an expert in esoterical works and a man keenly aware of the important goals of existence, writes:

> ''The word is energetic and authoritarian discourse. Combined with precise and constructive thought, with faith, words can cause a reversal of natural trends and heal a sickness, prevent an accident, perform what is improperly called a ''miracle'' when it is only the materialization of concentrated thought and constructive spoken words. Thus, this is in keeping with the promise: What you decree will be given unto you.''

Luck does not exist

Precious vibrations and powerful energies exist in the spoken word; they are astonishing to feel and to put into action. The assertion bears within it the power of wishes, promises and decrees. Luck does not exist. When we affirm: "I am really lucky", everything happens at matter's subtle level, as if we had made a "pact" with luck itself. The same type of energetic fusion obviously happens in the negative sense. Unfortunately, the result is often much more evident in the negative affirmation, since when such is the case, the spoken word is uttered absentmindedly, unconsciously, automatically and without the slightest effort. Under these conditions, the energetic fusion takes place much more easily. When we are aware of the power of our words, we become captain of the vessel of the body-spirit in which the soul travels. The thinker Fichte states:

> "The primordial source of all my thoughts and of all my life is not a foreign spirit; on the contrary, what I am is entirely of my personal creation. I want to be free signifies: it is I who will make of myself what I will."

Schmidt, the great master of dynamic psychology, has irrefutably established this reality and has used it to further all aspects of life. According to him, by the human being's power to determine what he will become, he becomes it. In this way, the human being is the undeniable master and the primeval cause of the circumstances and events which mark the entire course of his existence. His life is between his hands. For this reason, in Sanskrit he is called "*prabhu*" or master. This sublime responsibility is proof of his existential autonomy and **prohibits all claims he may lay with a so-called exterior master**, as is so often done out of sheer ignorance of the cosmic laws in Western religious systems and sometimes even in those of the East. The soul is the only cause of all that happens to it. By what means? Through the simple and terrible tool that is the word.

If "man digs his grave with his fork", as one old saying claims, he also forges his destiny with his tongue. The Gospel says: " It is what goes out of man's mouth which matters" and nothing else. Each word, each expression he utters determines a little more the circumstances which will crystallize in his life. What is absolutely tragic, and at the same time wonderfully magical, is the absolute nature of the process. It takes place when the words are pronounced unconsciously or automatically or even jokingly. Like a computer, the subconscious registers data without having the slightest sense of humour...

In his very beautiful analysis of the laws which govern the manifested world, Schmidt shows how luck does not exist. He writes:

> "When you say ''I am'', your thoughts are all ears because every ''I am'' is a call to accomplishment. Every thought related to an ''I am'', manifests an increasing tendency to accomplish and mobilizes the forces of growth or penury, failure or happiness. So that good alone manifests itself in your life, be careful that all sentences starting with ''I am'' are directed towards positive goals. ''I am sick, I am unhappy, I am tired, I am persecuted by destiny, I am poor, I am suffering, I am weak, I am in misery''; all are clear orders given to the powers of life to create the corresponding states or to develop them more deeply. If, on the contrary, you consciously say: ''I am free, I am strong, I am contented, I am always on top, I am fate's favourite, I am rich in successes, I am at one with the forces of good, I am conscious of God, I am destiny's ally, I am rich'', then more and more, these assertions will come to hold true. ''I am'' signifies: I am spirit born of the Divinity's spirit; I am a universal child and life's plenitude is mine in my own right. ''I am'', such is the name of the divine in you. Each time you express it consciously, you speak as God speaks, saying: ''Let it be'' to all that you assert."

Unhypnotising the subconscious

The nations who will successfully achieve the great harmony of the age of happiness will be those who play the music of their soul on the harp that is their language. Awareness of the spoken word – the song of destiny – constitutes the next step in humanity's evolution. The conscious affirmative word is a high-voltage regenerator and reharmonizer for material and subtle bodies, an inexhaustible source of strength for the physical and psychic natures. It constitutes the foundation of global health. It stimulates the fire of digestion, the organs' proper functioning. The little sentence ''I am in perfect health'', repeated in the serenity of the morning and in the tranquility of the evening, with the knowledge that what the new man decrees is already making its way towards him, can provide more well-being than any chemical product. Trying it is enough to convince one.

In the near future, when the healing power of sound will be better known, it will not be surprising to read at the bottom of a prescription the following note: medication should be taken with psycho-acoustic vibration: "I feel perfectly well, I am in excellent health" to be repeated ten times a day; morning, noon and evening...

Émile Coué, who revolutionized psychological automatism and shed great light on the far-reaching field of autosuggestion (by proving that imagination is always stronger than the will), treated, relieved and healed thousands of patients considered incurable by the school of medicine of the time. His treatment consisted in the repetition of a simple sentence: "Every day, in every way, I am getting better and better". Émile Coué understood the close relationship which exists between the vibratory energies of the word and psychological activity. In his view, suggestion only acts provided that it has been transformed into autosuggestion, in other words, provided it has been accepted.

What, then, ought we to accept? The verb "to suggest" comes from the Latin *suggerere*, which exactly signifies "to bear under". It is precisely this still mysterious force, hidden in the sound of words, held by the affirmative spoken word, which it is necessary "to accept", (the verb "to accept" comes from the Latin *acceptare*, which means to receive). What is accepted (received) becomes accessible... From this point on, autosuggestion can be used effectively to achieve therapeutic ends.

Like electricity, sound is a neutral energy; it can be either beneficial or malevolent. All depends on its use and generally, we are masters at practising harmful autosuggestion, without ever having taken lessons. Why does negative suggestion succeed so well? Because, it bears repeating, we practise it unconsciously, effortlessly. Some people automatically state: "I know that I will never succeed" or "I know that this or that catastrophe, this or that obstacle is insurmountable, unavoidable". They make these assertions without any particular effort. Therefore, the spoken words, and the power they hold, penetrate very easily into the subconscious, which accepts them. And since the latter regulates the functioning of our physical, psychic or moral being, it causes everything to happen in accordance with the order it has received. Persistent, but not rigid, repetition of a sound vibration contained in a positive sound-word can unhypnotise the negatively programmed subconscious and induce its creative mechanism to work not only in a positive sense, but towards higher states of consciousness.

Mantrasthetics: listening to the higher consciousness

In future years, this idea will be at the origin of a new science which will synthesize on the one hand, sound forces (music, speech, subliminal noises) and the power of autosuggestion, and on the other hand, the purifying effect of inspired meditative song. This new science could be called "mantrasthetics" (from the Sanskrit *manatatra*: liberating tool, and from the Greek *aisthêsie*: feeling). This system of knowledge will have as its objective sensitizing the human subconscious to the sound elements produced by the organs of the word (phoneme) which liberate the mental.

There already exists a Bulgarian method of accelerated training – "suggestology" – which uses music and rhythmic breathing to activate the brain's right hemisphere. But for the most part, autosuggestive methodologies are used to achieve goals related to the body and the conscious. "Mantrasthetics" will be directed towards modifying the conscious and awakening the soul.

To grasp the scope and effectiveness of such an approach, it is necessary to define the various roles played by the conscious, the subconscious and the unconscious or supra-conscious. The word unconscious is generally used to designate all that is beyond the conscious; that is why I prefer to call it **supra-conscious**.

The consciousness always trys to reason, to analyse logically and unfortunately, this quality often allows it to block the intuitive information that comes from the deepest part of ourselves. These profound intuitive perceptions stem from the supra-consciousness and are relayed by the subconscious.

We should not allow ourselves to be intimidated by intellectual sounding words which the authors of scientific works are all too fond of using. In reality, these concepts are extremely simple. To understand the close relationship between these three elements, one need only imagine that the **subconscious** is, in a manner of speaking, a postman whose work is to transmit messages from the central post office (the supra-consciousness) to the letter box (the conscious).

The **subconscious**, as an intermediary relay point, creates a bridge between the **supra-conscious** and the **conscious**. It is an intuitive half-consciousness. By the proper use of sounds, the practice of mantrasthetics provokes such states of relaxation that the **subconscious** has no other choice but to allow the **supra-conscious** to relay information. Thus, these "revelations" seep into the **conscious**! In fact, in certain states of relaxation or meditation, the inferior ego is in a condition of passivity. This is when the doors of the inner supra-conscious open. All sound perceptions, words, names, assertions, remarks, etc., accumulate in the supra-conscious. These "data" are collected and encoded without any real awareness on our part. Multiple sounds, conversations and pieces of music are stored inside the supra-conscious, which could be compared to a magnetic band where, among other things, is recorded all that the ear perceives in this life in addition to a portion of what it has previously perceived. In a sense, the supra-conscious is an accumulator of images, sounds, emotions, memories, directly connected to the manner in which we allow ourselves to perceive existence. The instant the individual's lifeforce is separated from the chemical elements which comprise its carnal form (a transition which is falsely called "death"), this accumulation of thoughts, desires and supra-conscious memories determines the conditions in which the human being will reincarnate itself. Therefore, pre-embryonic life (or anterior life) is simply a preparation for the present life, and the present life is itself the workshop in which are built the predispositions of all future life.

The realm of ecstasy

Seen from this angle, mantrasthetics could potentially have unimaginable consequences on human evolution, providing humankind with access to the supra-conscious memories carried from rebirth to rebirth. In order to perceive the song of the supra-conscious, it is keenly recommended that one enter a state favourable to the free circulation of energies between the supra-conscious and the conscious. The role of subliminal and relaxing music and above all, of listening to inspired meditative songs, can then prove to be of precious assistance. Indeed, the main quality of these songs is precisely to break down the barriers which rise up between the "post office" (the supra-conscious), the ''postman'' (the subconscious) and the ''letter box'' (the conscious).

Once these obstacles are obliterated, it is then possible for energies seeking only to circulate in both senses to flow freely, imparting on the entire being an equilibrium never achieved before. From this perfect equilibrium are born new sensations, such as invincible joy, serenity in the face of affliction, absolute trust in one's self and heightened perception of the Universal Intelligence. In the mantrasthetic gesture, the human being becomes a sensitive organ. What is ordinarily felt only by the ear spreads through the entire person and naturally becomes movement. The assimilated experience becomes dance, song, laughter, tears of joy and eventually, a global absorption into the realm of ecstasy. This ecstatic state is itself provoked by the perception of the unalterability of the soul and by the awareness of the immortal love relationship which unites this soul to the Primeval Essence.

A symphony of symbols

For the conscious, the sound of the word, the spoken word, is a symbol. What is this symbol? It is the idea expressed by a particular sound. The name of an object holds within it all the symbolic elements which are at the origin of the existence of the object it represents. This is why the sages of all eras and of all traditions have reached the same conclusion for millenia: **the world is music; the universe and all of creation are sound vibration**. When all the cells of the cosmos, all planets, all civilizations throughout the galaxy will vibrate in harmony, free from egotistic or anarchic desires, following the directives of the Great Universal Conductor by seeking the beauty of the whole – and not merely the pleasure of one minute part to the detriment of others – the immense cosmic symphony will be heard in all plains of existence and the living beings of all kingdoms will once again find the eternal rhythm of love, the celestial melody of the music of the soul. Such is the infinite goal of evolution.

The soul embodies the reality of the manifestation which appears to the eyes of the physical body in one form or another. The soul is the idea held within the symbol's form; it is the substance, and the ephemeral forms it takes through the nature of its desires constitute only various shadows of this substance. The melody never comes after the harmony, but the inverse. In the same manner, it is not the substance that comes after the shape, but the inverse. Since everything in creation tends to follow this pattern, the idea's manifestation tends to follow automatically its symbolized expression in the sound formula. This is why a state of peace occurs "around" the symbol-word peace, a state of health crystallizes "around" the word health, a climate of violence is felt where words symbolizing violence are frequently spoken. Success comes after the word success; wealth appears where the sentence "I am rich" is often repeated, etc.

In the esoterical tradition, the deity manifests itself and appears under the particular shape invoked by the musical energies contained in its multiple Names. A thousand different Names will eventually result in a thousand different apparitions, however, whether personified or not, all manifestations are manifestations of the same substance. If we take into account the physiological effects inherent in the emission of a given syllable, we realize that, through speech, **through the sung statement, words are taken in charge by the individual who pronounces them**. He takes possession of them and enters into a vibratory union with them, physically and psychically.

Another evolution

As the idea is confined within the sound symbol of the word, so is the soul imprisoned in the body. The spoken word is an idea in the making, ready to manifest itself in a given form, that is to say, to be materially formulated. This is what is generally called evolution, with the strange impression that evolution is the result of genetic mutation. Nothing is further from reality!

In this sense, Charles Robert Darwin's theory is faulty. Ronald Reagan, while still President of the United States, sensed this obvious inaccuracy; during an interview he declared: "The theory of evolution is a scientific theory like any other. Biologists no longer consider it as infallible as they did in the past. But if we must teach it in schools, we should also teach the Biblical version of Creation in schools."

The problem is a formidable one considering that the Bible is absent from the teachings that could have helped us: the Catholic Councils have made them disappear. In the year 553 AD, during the second Council of Constantinople, the thirst for immediate power pushed Byzantine Emperor Justinian to suppress from Christian Scriptures all teaching concerning reincarnation. Is this not the epitome of hypocrisy and dishonesty? But the West has accepted it and still accepts it in majority, blindly, or rejects the Bible without trying to understand it.

It is not the body which evolves, but the soul that inhabits it, through transmigration from one body to another. A musician can wish to play on a more advanced instrument; however, it is the musician who changes instruments and not the instrument which changes. By basing his theory of the evolution of species on the premise that a genuine genetic variation takes place from generation to generation, Darwin – and following in his footsteps, industrial civilization as a whole – rejected the archetype or the specific essence Plato referred to as "eïdos". It is this eïdos that may be said to be found in the sound of the word which represents it symbolically. It is the eïdos that evolves through the forms it takes on, the forms material nature agrees to lend it. Evolution does indeed occur, but not as Darwin understood it. Paradoxically, Darwin's hypothesis identifies a plan in nature, but does not enquire as to whom the planner is, which is absurd. As soon as one recognizes the existence of a plan, one must also recognize its creator, architect or designer. And if we claim that the great harmony of nature simply functions mechanically, should we not recognize that of necessity, there must exist an intelligent mechanical energy produced by a...Mechanic who makes it work? Visionaries call this primeval energy The Great Spirit, God, The Soul of the Universe, and scientific intellectuals, in an effort to be taken seriously, call it The Great Unifying Theory. Beyond these two visions, one Reality exists, awaiting in the silence of the eternal an elevated and purified humankind.

Behind the immense symphony of nature is the intelligence of a divine composer. To hear and interpret the music of the soul is to follow this creator's directives to perfection. This direction is precisely given by means of the creative word, this word which was in the beginning and by which all has been created. Man's spoken words have the power to symbolize the evolutionary idea of the divinity. Here, the verb ''to symbolize'' is taken in its classical sense, which means ''to agree with''. From this perfect agreement will be born the absolute creations by which man will recover the creative and therapeutic power of his voice.

The various physical aspects of the living being are neither a product of chance, nor the fruit of a hypothetical genetic mutation. They represent material nature's exact response to the desires of human beings. Through its own free will, the soul chooses to listen to a particular type of music, to pronounce certain words. Thus, it decides itself the circumstances and events of its evolution. By continuously surrounding itself with elevated sound vibrations, it creates the body of light it will inhabit in its future existence. By consciously immersing itself in an atmosphere charged with frequencies related to the hearing and the chanting of unlimited symbol-names designating the Primordial Cause, the soul rediscovers the memory of its foundation **and finds within itself (and not in the politics and bureaucracies of any exterior religion...)**, the strength to travel through the superior stages of its cosmic fulfillment.

CHAPTER 3

THE UNIVERSAL ENERGY OF MANTRAS

"Music is the universal language."

Richard Wagner

"Through the appropriate use of musical energies, not only can the human being eliminate mental blocks, he can also acquire, in his incorporal organic parts, a vibration superior to the one he knew before."

Pr. Zébério
Sounds and Human Energy

"Today, for powerful minds blinded by the science held in books and convinced that nothing can exist beyond what they know, all this does not make sense. "And nevertheless, it turns" as Galileo said, nevertheless patients are healed, the rain falls and the wind blows in the direction it has been decided upon. There are even spell-binding "words" which have the same effects."

Anne Osmont
The Creative Rhythm of Forces and Forms

"In the final analysis, it is true that each sound holds some mantric qualities."

Lama Anagarika Govinda
Creative Meditation and Multidimensional Consciousness

The highest premonition

Mantras are mentally liberating tools. They are not "magical formulae" whose function is to transcend cosmic laws or hypnotize the entity who chants or recites them. The goal of mantras is to awaken the lifeforces which exist in the human soul throughout eternity. Lama Anagarika Govinda defines them as:

> "archetypal sounds and verbal symbols which have their origin in the very structure of our consciousness. Thus, they are not arbitrary creations springing from an individual initiative; they are born from the collective or general human experience, modified only by cultural or religious traditions."

A mantra is therefore a symbol; according to Carl Jung, it is an idea which corresponds to the conscious being's highest premonition. The latter corresponds to the awareness of our divine nature. It is complete when it includes the consciousness of the Universal Soul within us and its unifying relationship with us. This union of devotion and love represents the quintessence of absolute happiness. The ultimate goal of the practice of mantras is precisely to recover this lost divine relationship.

The state of grace: a downward process

There are, of course, thousands of mantras with different functions, not related to this relational research. These mantras can serve to reach all kinds of goals which are more or less linked to material energy. However, the genuine goal of practising mantras is to connect oneself to the Divine. The process which leads to awareness of this relationship is not an upward process, but a downward one. In other words, these things are not born of a reflection in which the consciousness attempts to reach a spiritual level through intellectual effort. On the contrary, this awareness is a state of grace springing up from the depths of the heart. This state is offered, with no underlying motivation, by the medium of a master-guide. The mantric tradition is oral; the *shakti*, the energy, is passed from mouth to ear, from master to disciple. To receive a mantra from an authentic living master is, in itself, an initiation. This initiatory experience is a necessity for whomever wishes to follow the mantra's path, and it represents the beginning of its practice (*sadhana*). This initiation can also be experienced in a dream state as well as in a state of wakefulness.

The power of seed-syllables

The mantra's symbolic sound forms a bridge between superficial consciousness and the essential Ego located on the incorporeal level. On this plain, the structures of language as we know them disappear to give place to pure emotions and feelings, impossible to express through the verbal concepts used on physical plains. For this reason, most mantric formulae incorporate primary sounds without any precise meaning and which do not express any concept or idea. These are root-sounds or seed-syllables (*bija*). These root-sounds trigger the awakening of superior emotions by directly influencing the consciousness with vibrations whose resonances predate all human language.

In the Tibetan mystic, for example, we find the sound hùm which represents individuality and induces the descent from the state of universality to the depths of the human soul. The **u** is pronounced as it is in the English language. The stroke above the **u** extends the sound; the dot above the **m** indicates the mantric nature of the sound-seed and is said to turn back the sound towards the interior. The exterior vibration we hear is therefore transferred to the inaudible, but real, inner frequency. It is unnecessary to think about this or to try to reason it out. Similarly, when music or a song moves us, we cannot really explain why. **We simply feel something particularly powerful moving and evolving within us.** And we acutely feel that this energy moves the mountains of our indifference and insensitivity.

Exactly the same thing occurs with the seed-sound of a mantra. It is this inner frequency, inaudible to the physical ear, which actually holds the energy of the *bija*.

Immensity

This all-powerful energy is the *shabda*, or phonic group of letters which confers movement to sound. Without the perception of the *shabda*, or mystical sound enclosed in the mantra, which the initiate seeks to discover, the mantra's power cannot manifest its full strength. The sound *om* is the supreme *bija*. As the *hùm* is the descent of God towards the soul, the sound om is the opening of the soul to God and it corresponds to the ascent of individuality towards universality, towards the infinite. On this subject, the *Srimad Bhagavatam* says:

> "The sacred syllable *om*, vested with unsuspected powers, blooms like a lotus within the pure soul. It represents the Absolute Truth in its three aspects: impersonal reality, the Supreme Soul and the Supreme Being. All the Vedic resonances emanate from the sound *om*, which is begotten in the soul."

Countless pages have been written on the meaning and tenor of the sound *om* ; it is wise to read and assimilate them. However, it is even much more extraordinary to directly experience the power of *om*. In a comfortable position, let your body relax by breathing deeply. Once you are calm, pronounce the sacred mantra, without seeking to reason on it but merely by trying, with a simple heart, to feel its exceptional frequencies. In a few minutes, all metaphysical explanations are forgotten and become useless since we penetrate into the unsuspected realm of mystical experience. Here is sound, vibrant with joy and impregnated with love. The heart expands under irradiating warmth. The mind which, a few minutes before, painfully spun in all directions is catapulted in a single direction, concentrated, focussed on a point located at the centre of the heart. A ray of peace, illuminating the entire world, emanates from this point. Body and spirit are spontaneously bathed in an immense sense of gratitude. At one and the same time, we realize the power of the mantra and the stunning immensity of transcendental regions. He-who-does-not-dream, the awakened, the divine man, can then emerge from his old shell and can vibrate in harmony with the silent peace in which it is possible to perceive the sublime voice of his soul. When this hour comes, he knows that his dwelling is with the Omniscience; he remembers that physical life is but a theatre performance. From this point on, he no longer fears anything.

Beyond unconsciousness

While the repetition of a given sound architecture can provide well-being, fortune, health and all types of things, the ultimate goal of the practice of the mantra is to help us rediscover our spiritual identity. Through this awareness, we can reestablish the unique relationship that unites us to the living light of the God-Source. This rediscovery of the soul's life develops from listening (*shravana*). The entity who lends an attentive ear to mantric sound vibrations rapidly rids his heart of all impurity. The importance of listening is mentioned on several occasions in the revealed Scriptures. In the *Garuda Purana*, the *Vedic Scriptures* advocate the practice of listening in a very beautiful manner:

> "Existence conditioned by the universe of matter can be compared to the state of a man who lies unconscious, the victim of a snake's bite. These two forms of unconsciousness can both be dissipated by the vibrations of a mantra."

There are indeed given mantras capable of restoring life to someone who seems already dead from the serpent's bite and someone who, plunged into deep unconsciousness, remains in a type of comatose state. There are specific mantras capable of annihilating the venim's effects. In the comatose state as in the state of deep sleep, the ear is the only sensory organ still active; someone who seems already dead can still hear the sound that will save his life. Some shamans have mastered the art of using mantras and such exploits are not rare. Similarly, oblivion to the soul's existence has plunged the Earth into the deep sleep of indifference and insensitivity, the poisoned fruit of basest materialism. In the coma of illusion, the exchange of love between the divine spark and the divine Fire Being have been replaced by a pitiable sense of impersonality. In this state, nihilism and existentialism block the descent of great energies of light and peace, always ready to inundate the world. This is why sages perceive humanity as a transitory sphere plunged in the deepest darkness of ignorance, envy and hatred. Under the illusion of his restrictive egoïsm, man seems dead, though he vainly turns in all directions in search of a happiness which continues to elude him.

Profoundly listening to the revealed word

This lack of well-being can be healed by profoundly listening to all that is related to absolute truth. At least this is what is stipulated in the *Vedanta Sutra*:

> "He who wishes to be freed from all suffering, should hear what is related to God, should praise Him and keep in mind his personal aspect, Him, the Supreme Soul, the master and redeemer of all suffering." (*Srimad-Bhagavatam* 2.1.5)

The fire of inner life is therefore definitely lit and the living being, plunged in a state of unconsciousness by the illusive anxieties of his limited existence, comes out of his chronic lethargy and awakens in the world of his own divinity. The author of the *Vedic Scriptures*, Vyasadeva, describes the importance of listening to revealed Scriptures as they have been given (and will yet be given) to men through the words of countless masters of truth:

107

"It is essential to lend an attentive ear to the chants and sayings of the *acharyas* (model entities), which flow like rivers of nectar from their lunar-like faces. The soul which wholeheartedly listens to these spiritual sounds will undoubtedly see itself freed from hunger, thirst, fear and affliction and from all illusion related to the reductionist material consciousness." (*Bhagavatam* 4.29.40)

It is indeed through this consciousness of penury, in opposition to the consciousness of all-powerful plenitude, that are born most illnesses which eat away at first the spirit of men, and then their bodies.

Freedom from fear

Fear of penury, one's own afflictions and the world's, anxieties founded and unfounded, are rampant in the minds and hearts of human beings and create all sorts of negative thought-forms. These, of chaotic colours and shapes, are the factors underlying psychological disorders suffered by humankind. It has been proven that 80% of the illnesses treated by doctors are psychosomatic. When those who practise traditional medicine will broaden patterns limited to experimentation on animals and on physico-chemical laws, they will discover the science of autosuggestion.

Conscious or unconscious listening to the materially polluted sounds which saturate the modern world creates an overall autosuggestion of danger, penury and violence. Thus influenced, the subconscious is hypnotized by fear and life becomes a narrow space, minimized by an existential anguish based on a profound lack of intuitive knowledge. While this intuitive current is impaired by morbid anxieties, human beings fight for their existence, believing that the circumstances and events unfolding on the screen of their lives are the result of pure chance!

The human race halts its evolution by remaining shallow and fearful even though each individual it comprises is an heir to the spirit's limitless opulence and supra-natural powers. Fortunately, a great many doctors are currently beginning to emerge from the impass into which scholastic teachings have plunged them. On this topic,

Normand Cousin, a professor at the University of Los Angeles Faculty of Medicine, dares to state: "If I could give something to people, it would be to free them from their fears...because fear creates illness."

Thus, fear results in cellular disorders and listening to harsh, distressing sounds generates an autosuggestion of fear. Consequently, it comes as no surprise that listening profoundly to spiritual resonances releases the subtle energies of the soul and gradually destroys all that casts a shadow on the human beings' heart.

These mantric sound waves are a precious and powerful weapon in the already impressive arsenal of the new vibratory medicine which is, in fact – it should be noted – as ancient as Ayurvedic medicine. In an interview conducted by Michel Saint-Germain for *Guide Resources* Magazine, Dr. Richard Gerber provides a glimpse of a multidimentional human being with limitless healing potential. He states:

> "We tend to think that the human body is powered by electrophysiological forces (nerves, etc.), but this system is controlled by one of superior energies regulating cellular and biochemical processes. And this system of subtle energy is much closer in frequency to the lifeforce. Some forms of vibratory medicine are carried out at levels of what we refer to as elevated spiritual realities and which are not widely accepted by conventional science. Certain factions within the conventional scientific community believe this, but scientific institutions continue to reject these things, considering them to be eccentric... Medicine as a whole is changing because there are well-trained doctors who are gradually becoming interested in complementary approaches and who see these studies as more credible. These approaches are not intended to replace current scientific theory, but to extend it."

Whether it be crystals, sound vibrations, acupuncture, the astral body, floral essences, or...surgery, we must come to understand that all these approaches are in reality complementary; they are not opposed to one another. Healing amounts to freeing the body and mind from the negative energies which diminish them. The energy of mantras, phonic formulae whose vibratory effects exert a profound influence on our three main bodies (physical, mental and spiritual) can be successfully used in vibratory medicine and can immunize us against the anxieties at the root of most cellular imbalances.

Richard Gerber adds: "Healing is allowing the reestablishment of an overall creative movement: that of the body and the soul, that of the individual and the planet."

The way of song and listening

To listen to and sing spiritual sound vibrations while treading in the masters' footsteps constitutes for all the path to perfection and freedom from doubt and fear. This path is not only offered to students wishing to perfect their ideological research but also to those who have already triumphed in their efforts, whether they be the authors of interested acts, philosophers or lovers of the Essential Being (*Bhakti-yogis*). This path of listening and song is not affected by age, race, sex or social status. It is free, easy, without any strict rules concerning place or time. The pleasure of singing and listening to the sound of mantras progressively awakens within us. This method is not only reserved to those who wish to succeed in self-realization practices, it is equally recommended for anyone who is attached to material life. All the masters of Vedic science agree that this is a sure path to perfect success.

The enigma of living repetition

Individuals who have failed to assimilate properly the strength released by the phenomenom of repetition sometimes criticize the practice of mantras. It should be recognized that this criticism is based on insufficient knowledge of the science of mantra and on incomplete experimentation of **active musical repetition**. On this subject, musicologist George Balan says:

"The message of sound is an enigma to our mind. He who feels that this enigma hides the key to spiritual liberation will obviously strive to solve it. The only way to do so is to repeat the melody until a symbiosis is achieved. This is a living repetition, and has nothing of the mechanic in it. Success is achieved only by letting the music reverberate within one's self as consciously as possible. The more the melody is interiorized, in other words, sung not so much with the lips as with the inner voice, the more it will permeate our depths, making them radiate. When practised diligently, slowly but surely, this repetition will bring with it the solution to the enigma, a solution of a nature totally different from the solution arrived at through reasoning and sensed as a considerable increase in our psychic strength. This intimate work is nothing more than the musical expression of the laws underlying all authentic meditation, namely the confrontation of the enigma, which in the Zen tradition is called "koan" and the "digesting" of the meditation formula, better known under the Sanskrit word *mantram*, whose action on the soul can make of man a new Oedipus, conqueror of the inner Sphinx, source of agonizing enigmas."

Thus, the repetition of a given sound formula is not an obstacle, rather, it is of precious assistance provided, of course, that it is not repeated mechanically or automatically. It is absolutely essential that the heart be entirely available and actively engaged in the repetition of the chant. If only the lips are involved and if the mind wanders, the heart will remain empty and will find within itself neither the strength nor the desire to taste the mantra. This tasting – which has nothing at all in common with the pleasures of the senses or of the flesh, being far superior in intensity and quality – is the direct result of repetition, provided the latter is conscious and living. Anyone who sincerely sets out on the royal path of repetition of the mantras must expect to experience sooner or later a joy which goes beyond and transcends all joys. His entire life may consequently be transformed. This experience does not belong exclusively to the Sanskrit culture.

In the *Philocaly*, one of the most complete and inspired works on the topic, are found several allusions to this inexpressible superior pleasure which is born of prayer from the heart. In the *Philocaly* – which Nicodemus described as the safeguard of intelligence and the infallible guide to contemplation – Isaac de Ninive, an extraordinary monk of the 9th century, writes of the superior and mystical pleasure that springs from the repetition of his own mantra-prayer, the famous prayer of Jesus: "Lord Jesus Christ, have pity on me, Son of God."

"He who suceeds in continuous prayer attains all virtues and at the same time, finds a spiritual dwelling. Whether he is asleep or awake, prayer never leaves his soul. While he eats, drinks, lies down, works, sleeps, the perfume of prayer is spontaneously exhaled from his soul. One should not confuse the joy of prayer with the vision of prayer: the latter is stronger than the former. It sometimes happens that the chant of words is particularly smooth on the lips and that the same word is repeated endlessly without creating a feeling of satisfaction required to go beyond and onto the next word. Sometimes, the repetition of sacred words leads to a degree of contemplation and the prayer dies on the lips. He who experiences such contemplation enters into the realm of ecstasy. This is what we refer to as the vision within prayer, it is not an image or a shape invented by the imagination, as inexperienced fools claim.''

A feeling of light

This state of ecstasy, this superior pleasure, is the ripened fruit of the music of the soul. When the therapeutic effect of sounds combines with the effects of words, we witness the emergence of a supranatural feeling. This feeling, which transcends mere sentimentality, is of a spiritual nature and it can enlighten the entire being in so far as it makes possible harmonic fusion with the source of all light. At this moment, the distinct soul can perceive the inconceivable music of forgotten worlds, remembering the pure Love relationship which unites it with the great heavenly families. Unified, it recovers its immense powers and sings in unison with the whole of creation. This is what prompted Father Mersenne to write in his *Universal Harmony*, published in 1636:

> "The spirit begins to enjoy the music of the blessed when it hears the unison which causes it to recall its origin and the bliss it hopes for and awaits."

The mysteries of harmonic frequencies

In spite of sceptics who believe that the sound wave acts on a psycho-physiological level, as do all derivatives of attention, musicologist Washco indicates that the more melodic and rhythmic elements are defined in a harmonic combination, the more precise will be the physiological reactions they trigger and the more we can be assured of their manifestation. It should be noted, however, that depending on the listeners' emotional state, the same musical energies produce very different physiological reactions.

What is the mechanism at the origin of these reactions in body and mind? Researcher La Monte Young puts forward a hypothesis as interesting from the point of view of music in general as it is from that of the sound vibrations involved in the incantations of ancient traditions. This hypothesis provides a rational explanation for the mysterious effect of sung mantras or of prayers used throughout all time, in all parts of the planet, by peoples conscious of the power of sound. According to him:

> "When a specific series of harmonically related frequencies is continuous, in a more definite way it produces or stimulates a psychological state which is felt by the listener given the fact that such a series of frequencies will continually trigger a specific series of auditory nerves which, in turn, will carry out the same transmission operation from a periodic model of impulses to the series of points determined by their counterparts in the cerebral cortex."

In light of this idea, we cannot help but think of the famous Hindu *raga* whose exact scales are said to provoke always the same effects. Edith Lecours, who studied La Monte Young's hypothesis in the course of in-depth research on the actuality and development of musicotherapy, believes that this idea could also be applied to other musics said to be "primitive", where the therapeutic function finds its precision and its circumspection in the use of sounds, in so far as these sounds are properly prolonged and in so far as they permeate the individual as is the case, for example, of Tibetan songs.

Om mani padme hum: the healing compassion

Scholars of the soul are unanimous in saying that among other effects, these syllables produce compassion. While there is a measure of the multidimensional in mantric formulae, it seems that it is mainly the energies of compassion which result from the listening to, or the chanting of, this combination of seed-syllables and word-symbols. This mantra has often been translated by the sentence: "Oh thee, Jewel in the lotus"; but in my opinion, mantras should not be adapted to current language by philosophical interpretations. They are what they are, and the energy that emanates from them should above all be felt physically, psychically or spiritually rather than being intellectually analyzed through the means of reasoning.

To illustrate this particular point, I cannot but think of the bumble-bee. Indeed, according to mathematical theory, the bumble-bee should not be able to fly since its body is not proportionate to its wing-span. But the bumble-bee laughs at mathematics and flies freely. It relies on its instinct, not on reason. Mantras resemble the bumble-bee: they are not reasonable. They put aside the intellect and **function simply by liberating the energies which correspond to the resonances they carry**. Hence, if we wish to understand the sound formula, we have no physical means other than basic experience and the experience of the multiple associations of the mysterious forces contained in their word-symbols. The energy of mantras simply cannot be understood in any other way. Rather than wondering how it is mathematically possible to fly, would we not be better off saving precious time, opening the doors of our minds and flying on the wings of sound, propelled by the reactors of mantric light towards the invisible dimensions of existence?

This being said, it is likely that in light of the data compiled by La Monte Young, in the near future some laboratory research will be undertaken and researchers will discover that a given mantra – a specific series of harmonically related frequencies – can indeed produce a specific psychological state, this state being triggered by the stimulation of a particular series of auditory neurons which, in turn, transmit a certain combination of impulses to the corresponding point in the cerebral cortex. We will then better understand how a given sound can result in a given psychological or physical state. Thus, the mantra "*om mani padme hum*" leads to a feeling of compassion, automatically followed by general well-being characterized by a relaxed body and a mind at peace.

In his book entitled *The Mantras or the Power of Sacred Words*, John Blofeld writes:

"Everywhere I went in these mountains (Tibet), the efficiency of the mantra *om mani padme hum* was proven to me! it acted as a protective spell...For the non-initiate, "*Mani*" is often used as a spell to ward off all types of misfortune. It is recited aloud as a protection against danger, recited softly to comfort someone in affliction, recited mentally or aloud without interruption for rebirth in the pure earth. Countless are the Tibetans who recite the *Mani* on their death-beds. Recently, Professor Charles Luk (in Chinese Lu K'uan-Yu), a remarkable researcher and writer and an authority on Chinese Buddhism, wrote to me to draw my attention to the therapeutic qualities of the mantra in cases of psychic illnesses such as hallucinations and other similar disorders. The patient must practise daily. I myself was healed within one evening from an illness I had contracted on one of my trips in the mountains of North China. Having fallen from my mule because I suddenly began to feel faint, people from the nearest inn had come to my rescue. There, I sank into a deep comatose state. When I regained consciousness, a Mongol lama standing at the foot of my bed was reciting in a low voice the *Om Mani Padme Hum*. The result was wonderful! Pain and fatigue disappeared and the following morning, I was as bright and lively as I had been on the very first day of my journey. Of course, in such circumstances, it is easy to argue that the mantra's beneficial effect is solely psychological, a point I do not contest; but things are not as simple as they may appear to be. For the energy of compassion personified by Avalokiteshvara is very real and lies hidden in the recesses of consciousness. Present in each of us although strongly restrained by the ego's shortcomings, it can be set in motion by the syllables of the mantra, particularly if they are recited with an altruistic goal. In spite of appearances, no magical operation is involved. The mantra – psychically related to an identical element in the psyche of those it is used for – draws enormous strength from the power accumulated over the course of centuries by sacred groups involving numberless practitioners.''

Sound penetrates the omnipresent ether

The word is a gift from He through whom all lives, the Sat (absolute existence) of which we are the infinitesimal living particles. This divine quality, this incomparable gift, is the origin of all human creation. Give a name to a being or an object and the being will exist, the object will manifest itself on the subtle plains of ether. Sound is not spread at the level of air, but of ether. This is why the sound, the word, the name, born of the mother-word, penetrates all things, ether being the omnipresent subtle element on the physical plain. Consequently, if we continue to name an object, a particular quality or a being, the latter will manifest itself in matter. This creative process is, in fact, a question of continuity.

In the Buddhist *Vajrayana doctrine*, the bija-mantra **ah** – corresponding to the letter A, the first in our alphabet – represents the mystery of the spoken word (*vak*). This mystery goes beyond that of the ordinary word. It is the audible symbol through which man expresses himself and it holds the power to transmit the work of truth. It is creative sound, the initiatory language which rekindles the spark of real spiritual light at the bottom of the heart of the radiant being, the happy and essentially immortal entity. The letter A, word of mystery, holds the secret of the creative sound energy of images, dreams, visions, thoughts – indeed, of all that is related to art, culture and science. This mystery of the word is more than divine, it is the Universal Intelligence Itself. This assertion is corroborated by the *Vedic Scriptures*.

Krishna asserts before Arjuna in His *Song of the Blessed: aksaranam akaro'smi* – ''Among all letters, I am the A'' (Bhagavad-Gita 10.33). *Akara*, the first letter of the Sanskrit alphabet, constitutes the beginning of all Vedic literature. No word can be pronounced without it. The letter A represents the origin of all sound. And the sound, or the word, is God Himself. *Sabdah khe paurusam nrsu* (Bhagavad-Gita 7.8):

''I am the infinite which sustains all. I am the sound within ether.''

This verse confirms the fundamental idea according to which the unbegotten light (or ''black'' for the human intellect) manifests its omnipresence by means of sound penetrating the etherial element, found at the origin of all Creation.

Perceiving the absolute

It is possible to perceive the Divine Presence through its countless sound energies and thus to realize Its impersonal aspect. The impersonalist, for instance, will be content to perceive the Absolute in the sound born by ether everywhere in the galaxy. But the personalist, on the other hand, will not neglect to glorify the Absolute Being for allowing human beings to express their feelings, emotions, thoughts, joys and sorrows through the extraordinary means of the spoken word, music and song. Here is recognition of the Absolute in all its aspects: impersonal, personal and localized. *Pravanah sarvavedesu* (Bhagavad-Gita 7.8)

"Of Vedic words, I am the sacred syllable **om.**"

The **om,** also referred to as *omkara and pravana*, or the spiritual sound vibration addressed to the Supreme Being and which begins all Vedic incantations, emanates from Him. The impersonalists, frightened at the very idea of being absorbed in God by the chant of his countless Names, prefer to hear the vibration of the sound of the *omkara*, failing to understand that it is also the sound representation of the Supreme Elohim. In fact, personalism and impersonalism are not in opposition. **These two aspects of truth are perfectly complementary**. For those who know the *causa-causarum* and all that it is, has been and will be, all things involve at one and the same time the personal and the impersonal, as, moreover, is taught in the sublime Caitanyan doctrine of the *achintya-bhedabheda-tattva*: simultaneous Unity and multiplicity.

A.U.M.: the key to transformation

The manner in which sound can give us the opportunity to contact transcendental realities is clearly established by Swami Bhaktivedanta in his commentary on the *Vedanta-Sutra*. In the second part of this impressive work of esoterical and devotional literature, Chapter 1, Verse 17 reads as follows:

> "*Abhyasen manasa suddham*
> *trivrd-brahmaksaram param*
> *mano yacchej jita-svaso*
> *brahma-bijam avismaran*"

117

This signifies: "After sitting down in a remote and pure place, the seeker must bring his thoughts back to the three absolute letters (A.U.M.) and, by regulating his breathing, must master his mental processes in order not to forget this spiritual key."

Om, the *pravana*, the *omkara*, the sacred syllable formed by three absolute letters – A.U.M. – (*suddham tri-vrt*) is the key, the seed of intimate self-realization. Reciting it mentally while regulating one's breathing – a spiritual technique created and practised by great yogis and through which one achieves a state of profound oxygenation – makes it possible to master mental processes dominated by the ways of matter. Swami Bhaktivedanta explains that in this way, it is entirely possible to cure oneself of harmful mental habits.

Certain schools of meditation teach that it is necessary to "kill" the mental. This is a serious mistake! Indeed, regardless of the method used in doing so, nothing is more harmful than attempting to suppress mental activity and the being's desires. Yet more often than not, this is what is attempted in misguided yoga centres (*ashram*)...

It is important to realize that mental activity and desire cannot be halted. It is, however, possible to cultivate the desire to act in light of the goal of ultimate evolution. It is vain to try to "kill" the mental. Rather, it is the very nature of the object of the thought itself that should be transformed.

Bhaktivedanta points out:

> "Since the mental represents the pivot, the axis which directs the active organs, if we transform the nature of mental functions – thinking, feeling and wanting -- the activity of the senses will be modified accordingly. Only the spiritual sound is capable of bringing forth the desired mental and sensory transformation and the omkara A.U.M. forms the first seed, the key to all spiritual sound vibration. The power of spiritual sound is such that it can even heal those who suffer mental imbalance."

The Vedic text is clear on the subject of this extraordinary vibration – the *Sri-Caitanya-caritamrta, Adi-lila* and Chapter 7, Verse 128 states:

> "*prandva' se mahavakya – vedera nidana isvara – svarupa pranava sarva' va-dhama*".

This means: "The Vedic sound vibration Om (*omkara*), the most important word in all of Vedic literature, is the basis of all vibrations. Therefore, it should be accepted as the sound representation of the God-Source's sublime personality and should be perceived as the trustee of all cosmic manifestations."

Nothing less! However, Khrisna himself does not hesitate to declare (*Bhagavad-Gita 8.13*):

> "*Om ity ekaksaram brahma*
> *vyaharam mam anusmaran*
> *yah prayati tyajan deham*
> *sa yati paramam gatim*"

This verse indicates that OM is the direct representation of God. If, at the moment of physical death, we can simply remember this unique mantra, we leave our body with the memory of the Divine Presence and consequently, we are immediately transferred to spiritual plains.

In the next chapter (The initiatory emotion of Sacred Names), we will see how powerful are the different appellations of the Supreme Divinity. Nevertheless, the sincere student who understands that the *omkara* is the sound representation of the divine, will realize that the power of Om, sung in light of this awareness, is in all aspects identical to the power of Holy Names (Buddha, Yahwe, Jehovah, Allah, Krishna, Cristos, Adonaïs, etc., etc.).

In his thesis, the *Bhagavat-sandarbha*, the holy philosopher Jiva Gosvami asserts that Om is considered to be the sound vibration of the divine name. Only this vibration can deliver the soul from the claws of universal holographic illusion (*Maya*). The great commentator Sridhara Swami describes the *omkara* as the seed of deliverance from the physical worlds.

The reforming avatar Caitanya stipulates in his teachings that *Omkara* holds all the powers of the Absolute and is in no way different from God. To sing it amounts to directly encountering the Personality of the Creative Forces of the universe in its sound form.

The *Mandukya Upanishad* declares that what it is possible to perceive on spiritual plains is nothing short of an extension of the absolute power of Om.

Finally, the Goswamis, the sages of Vedic culture, provide a detailed explanation of Om by analyzing it according to the terms of its alphabetical constituents:

a – Karenocyate krsnah
      sarva-lokaika-nayakah
u – karenoeyate radha
      ma-karo jiva-vacakah

Omkara is a combination of the letters A, U and M. The letter A refers to the Friend of all living entities and the Ruler of all material and spiritual planets. According to the science of mantras, it is the static wave. The letter U indicates the power of divine pleasure (*Srimati Radharani*) or the wave of resonance. The letter M indicates living beings. It is the oscillating wave, marginal energy.

Impersonalist philosophers (*mayavadis*) consider several Vedic mantras as *maha-mantra*, or "great" mantra. According to the *Bhagavad-Gita*, most of these mantras are in fact only accessories. However, the *omkara* can be considered a *maha-vakya* or *maha-mantra*, non-differentiated from God. Such a realization cannot be proven in a laboratory setting and is possible only by simply chanting the Sacred Name of the Divine Presence, *Omkara*.

This combination of sound vibrations (A.U.M.) has not been invented or "fabricated" by a human being. In reality, this "transcendental" sound possesses a spiritual and absolute power and by singing and listening to its particular harmonics, we realize that this power **is Divine Mother-God (as total Unifying Energy) in all its aspects.**

OM, the music of the spheres

The *Omkara* is identical to what we sense as God. This presence cannot be seen or heard by imperfect senses. Such is the genuine illness of the conditioned being.

Training based on a technique of respiratory mastery combined with a silent, inner recitation of the *Omkara* is essential for anyone who wishes to see spiritual realizations appear in the mental, where all sensory activities reside.

Chanting and listening to the *Omkara* are the first steps towards spirtitual enlightenment. In general, we suffer from an incomplete perception of the universe. We are incapable of realizing the Forms or Sublime and Personal Names of the Absolute because our senses are impaired by matter. As long as this state persists, it is impossible for us to concentrate our thoughts directly on the personal aspect of truth. By following the impersonal discipline which consists of listening and chanting the *Omkara*, the mental gradually frees itself from all preconceived ideas which weigh it down and we are able to contemplate the personal features of the all-powerful and all-loving hidden presence.

Progressively, spiritual sound succeeds in removing the mental from sensory activities. This sound vibration sustains the power of intelligence which is then able to control the senses. Hence, the mental gradually loses the habit of being absorbed in solely material action. However, be this as it may, it does not sink into sterile inactivity since it eventually suceeds in embracing the service of love offered to the Divine Omnipresence and in fully establishing itself in a perfect state of consciousness.

A purifying process

This service of love is manifested by listening, chanting and remembering what is related to the common cosmic Eternal Father-Mother in any of its multiple personal representations (*sravanam kirtanam vishnou smaranam*) and is established in the perfect ecstasy, the *samadhi*, representing the highest degree of the previously prescribed method.

Experience shows us that even the state of *samadhi* proves to be inefficient when it comes to mastering a mental process absorbed in matter. The story of a great number of yogis bears witness to this truth. The mental, although it momentarily ceases to think about the activities of the senses, recalls past actions which spring from the subconscious and create an obstacle for the soul which wishes to dedicate itself to spiritual realization. This explains the importance of the direct method of listening and chanting the mantric Names of the Sovereign Essence.

In many instances, the Vedic Scriptures stipulate the superiority of this method. They designate it as *"yoginam"*, the surest path to spiritual emancipation. Even human beings experiencing mental turmoil are ensured of progress if they take this path under the direction of a qualified teacher (*guru*). Thus the impersonal spiritual sound vibration (the *Omkara*), quintessence of all mantras, leads us to the shores of the Sacred Names of the Primeval Essence, root of the seven cosmos.

Chanting these mantras, more specifically the Om, holds the power to clean the interior. This purification process eliminates from the mental all karmic dust accumulated in the past. The results of the chant can be perceived directly, without an intermediary. Even if it be for only a few minutes daily, whoever chants or listens to one or several of these countless words of power sooner or later feels a transcendental pleasure and is rapidly purified from material contamination. In the three worlds, there is no medicine more powerful than the Sacred Names. The active influence of their sound sequences, which can be emitted through the intermediary of human language, represents the perfect tool for awakening the soul.

Music: the physics of the soul

In Dr. Deepak Chopra's revolutionary book *Quantum Healing* (Exploring the Frontiers of Mind / Body Medicine, Bantam Books 1989, a work I recommend to all those who wish to know more on the therapeutic power of primordial sounds), one can read "*finer subatomic particles would seem to be waves of form, vibrations called "superstrings", or supra-sensitive chords, because they react in exactly the same way as the strings of a violin...*". These *superstrings* develop everywhere in the universe and their number is infinite. They underlie all creation. Since this subatomic network is located beyond the limited reality of our four dimensions, no current laboratory instrument, regardless of how powerful, can observe them.

This very recent theory of physics is surprisingly close to the Vedic text which stipulates that all cosmic transformation is supported by a Creative Power, much as the pearls of a necklace are threaded on a string.

Thus, nothing is inert, nothing is isolated. Everything vibrates interactively. Each organ is sustained by a particular "superstring" which must be well tuned, otherwise the organ will play out of tune. Therefore, we can no longer consider the body to be a mass of inert flesh; the Ayurvedic vision shows us that it is a network of "*sutras*", or conductive wires. The body is a sound box.

The best way to act upon a vibratory frequency consists mainly in emitting a corresponding vibratory frequency using the well-known phenomenom of resonance.

This explains, for instance, the success obtained by Dr. Desikachar who directs an institute in Madras (India) where Ayurvedic medicine, yoga and song are taught. The institute is mentioned in a brilliant document written by Cécile Beaudet and Richard Belfer, "Healing Music" (La musique qui soigne) (*L'Impatient*, June 1989, No. 139), recognized as in the public good by the Department of Health. Dr. Desikachar points out:

> "Our ancestors had classified the letters of the alphabet in different categories. Certain sounds, HA with an aspirated H, for example, have a stimulating effect. Others, like MA, sung softly in a low-pitched note, have a calming effect."

Cécile Beaudet and Richard Belfer say that this knowledge has led the institute's teachers to use song with pregnant women (as a preparation for delivery), with asthmatics (to help them exhale), with people suffering from hypertension (to help them relax) and with individuals who suffer from backaches (to correct both their breathing and their posture).

In their document, the authors also quote Jill Purce, therapist and voice coach who, in the course of her work with Stockhausen and the Tibetan Buddhist masters, discovered that:

123

"A great many of our contemporaries are dissatisfied with their life and feel that another part of themselves could be developed. In such a case, healing – for patients – does not necessarily involve working directly on the symptom. I consider illness to be *the expression of a more deeply rooted imbalance* which must be corrected. For each of us, each moment can bring with it the pretext to regret the past or to fear the future. Because of this anxiety, things are less and less similar to what we expect. Depending on our weak points, this disequilibrium will manifest itself in the form of a cold, a backache or a cancer."

This desequilibrium is also a series of false notes, a cacophony, mental at first, then cellular. What should be done, then, is to calm our mental agitation in order to act on the organism, where mantric energies are genuinely useful and are even irreplaceable. This is the reason why a Tibetan master can suggest meditative exercices which will lead us to visualize a letter, or a series of letters, a *mantra*, and then to sing it. By chanting the mantra (or listening to it) we feel a vibratory effect which calms mental activity, often overwhelming and uncontrollable, to then act directly on specific parts of the body.

As Dr. Richard Gerber (author of *Vibrational Medicine*, Bear and Co. Publishers) stated so accurately in the course of an interview conducted by Michel Saint-Germain (*Resource Guide*, Vol. 5, No. 2, Nov.-Dec. 1989):

"We already use vibratory medicine without realizing it: all these forms of treatment are based on energy. The medical establishment is not aware of the fact that it already calls upon energy in the course of the healing process. *Ultrasound is already used to dissolve kidney stones: this is sound energy, vibratory medicine.*"

Sound (like electricity and light) is a conventional form of electromagnetic energy; if used in harmony with the subtle energy of the consciousness (activated with effective mental visualization combined with the power of creative assertion), in a sense, this form of energy becomes "all-powerful" since it is transmitted to the deepest oscillations of the organism through the vector of the "superstrings". Sound is the surgeon's new scalpel, but this is a scalpel which knows nothing of pain, which involves none of the dangers of general anaesthetics; moreover, it is more pleasant to submit oneself ("to put oneself under") musical energies than to yield one's body, often in blind faith, to the hands of those who still practise medicine with the heavy artillery of modern surgery.

Thus, vibratory energy partly justifies the results obtained by using the therapeutic power of music and mantras. This subatomic sound current being retroactive, the superstring network also explains why the *Bhagavad-Gita* defines the Source-Principle as "the sound which traverses ether." This is the omnipresence which sustains all. At this level, there are no religious concepts (in the Catholic or Hindu sense of the word); there is an intuitive vision, knowledge, application of what has been "seen" by a millenary tradition as well as by scientific experimentation (quantum physics, micro-vibratory physics, vibratory medicine, etc.). This physical omnipresence of subatomic particles, vibrating and dancing, which physicist Fritjof Capra so rightly compares to the dance of the god Shiva, enlightens us on how primitive man (whom I qualify as original man and not "primary" man, as conventional education continues to describe him) felt and understood the following: this man, supposedly primitive, prehistorical, while imitating the natural sounds of his environment, vested himself with the power of the lifeforces at the source of these sounds. Science has not yet "discovered" the subtle effect of retroactive waves. Hence, primary man was not as low on the evolutionary scale as we were led to believe.

This opinion is shared by Dr. Thérèse Brosse, long-time director of the cardiology clinic of the Paris Faculty of Medicine. In a letter addressed to researcher Maud Forget, she writes:

> "There is no doubt that prehistorical man had direct knowledge of these things owing to the fact that the evolutive strategy which eventually walled us behind an inexorable mental process had not yet affected him."

It could not be better expressed.

Conscious electromagnetic sound energy forms the foundation of the ritual songs and dances of the American Indian civilization's shamans and medicine men. This same energy was used during the Brahman ceremonies of the Vedic culture and in Egyptian initiations during which major phonic formulae and powerful sound and mantric structures were sung and heard. Today, particle accelerators have led to the discovery of a supersensitive network – or current. We have a better understanding of how mantras can trigger vibratory effects which have a far-reaching influence at the atomic and subatomic levels of the physical, psychic and...spiritual. Egyptians called music, the "physics of the soul". Far be it from Dr. Chopra, for whom DNA is the messenger of the quantum world, to contradict them. It was through this infinite network of superstrings that, for mythologists, Orpheus restored life to Eurydice thanks to the harmonius sound of his harp and the gentle power of his voice. In the same way, according to legend, the musician-surgeons of Atlantis healed their patients.

Dr. Frank Alper is not an archeologist. He is the founder of the Arizona Metaphysical Society and is a well-known lecturer on metaphysics in the United States. In his work *Exploring Atlantis* (Arizona Metaphysical Society, Phoenix, 1981), Dr. Alper describes what the Atlanteans called the "Temple of Sound". Inside this pyramid-shaped building with walls of light, the Atlanteans raised their molecular vibrations by singing certain series of sounds. Dr. Alper does not hesitate to compare this language to the ancient Hebrew language which, according to him, is derived from the vocal vibrations used in the first days of Atlantis. Some of these songs have not been heard on earth for millenia. To emphasize the universality of sound processes, Dr. Alper writes thus on the structure *"yo-ooh-daa"*:

> "This song symbolizes the number ten and the number one, which corresponds to the "Yod" in the Hebrew alphabet. The "Yod" represents the force of the Universe; this letter is thus extremely powerful and is a very exalted spiritual song or sound."

Further, Alper adds:

> "It is important to understand that sound vibrations serve exactly the same purpose as a tuning-fork. As soon as it touches your skin, its pulsations are deeply felt."

Dr. Alper's works, particularly *Exploring Atlantis*, Vols. 1, 2 and 3, are extremely clear on the therapeutic use of sounds, colours and crystals (vibratory medicine) in the Atlantean initiatory tradition[1].

---

1. Twenty-four of these Atlantean therapeutic songs have been recorded and are available through the Head Office of the Arizona Metaphysical Society (P.O. Box 44027, Phoenix, Arizona 85069). Sung by Dr. Alper himself, these songs have a very real therapeutic power. The credit for rediscovering these universal songs is his. An artistic but less complete version of these Atlantean healing sounds is given on the yang side of the Atlantis Angelis recording (Atlantis Angelis, Healing Sounds, A-3318, No. 73 Aura-Musick).

These sound rituals or mantras are the means through which a given vibratory force is transmitted to an organ, a muscle, a vertebra, a thought, through the subtle subatomic particle vector. By providing the whole body (physical, emotional, etherial) with a perfect harmonic vibration, such as the primordial sound OM, for example, it is possible to fine tune the musical instrument which represents our organism as a whole.

In her ground-breaking book, *From Sound Springs Light* (Du son jaillit la lumière), Hélène Caya writes:

> "The listening techniques of inner resonance and realignment remain first and foremost a means to prevent serious disturbances within the organism. Ideally, each day we would go about, checking on the small disorders which, like intruders, disturb our peace and equilibrium."

This is exactly what is done by a person who hears or listens to a mantric meditative song, whether consciously or not; whether it be a song from Atlantis, Egypt, India, America, Africa or from another planet, is only relatively important. Above all, what counts is a better grasp and application of this "quantum" music (or in other words, the primordial, creative and archetypal sounds of the Universe) which acts at the atomic cellular level and at the thought level (cells and thoughts being nothing more, it should be recalled, than vibrating energy).

Each day, at home, or on a regular basis in workshops, it is possible to reharmonize one's mind and one's body through sound – preventive and therapeutic action.

This overall harmonization affects cardiac rhythm, blood circulation, breathing, and digestion as well as directly affecting the glands, extraordinary organs whose function is to produce secretions and which play an important role in our psychic and spiritual equilibrium.

A little more than fifty years ago, no one knew the endocrinal glands existed; however, the sages of Vedic civilization were well aware of their existence. Each gland, according to the *Vedic Scriptures*, has a vibratory frequency which coincides with that of a *bija-mantra*, that is to say, a primordial sound (seed-sound or root-sound). Each gland corresponds to a state of consciousness which is itself localized in a "centre" or chakra. We will come back to this point. In the following section of this book, we propose an exercise in which the centres of consciousness are retuned to the proper frequency. It is not necessary to understand intellectually the functioning of this kind of millenary exercise, which put into practice the fundamentals of vibratory medicine. Atlanteans practised a similar exercise in their Temple of Sound. Egyptians adopted the same practices in their monastery-clinic called the Temple of Beauty.

Whether or not we can analyze the precise nature of fire through logic, it continues to burn. In the same way, sound has an effect. The state of fulfilment and health it provokes when methodically applied endures the test of any thorough scientific examination for the simple and obvious reason that it does indeed have an effect...

Figures illustrating the sound method known as psychophony published in Marie-Louise Aucher's book *Sonorous Man* (L'Homme sonore) [a method patented by the Paris Academy of Science] show a marked similarity between the points in the body which vibrate in harmony with certain notes and the points used in acupuncture. When asked how a psycophonic sound test and acupuncture are related, Marie-Louise Aucher replies:

> "The Chinese have named the outline of acupuncture points: "The governing vessel which is in command of psychological and physical lifeforces", resonance zones are related to points of assent (a "point of assent" is "a harmonic junction point"). Acupuncturists activating these points with their needles have recognized and used these harmonic relationships over the course of centuries."

In the following exercises, instead of using metal needles, it is with soft sound waves that the chakras, the energy of centres of harmonic junction, will be made to vibrate.

For instrumentalists, and to give one last detail on the experimental use of musical notes related to mantras, it is preferable to respect the Pythagorian scale (A3 = 432 frequencies).

In 1953, at an international conference held in London, it was *arbitrarily* decided that the official value of LA should be raised, and set at 440 Hz. What prompted the decision to raise the official frequency of LA, already too high at the time (at 435 Hz)? Apparently no one knows... Is this not the height of carelessness?

What strange reasoning brought about this change in traditional musical harmony, which has always been founded on the rigorous observation of the rhythms of Nature? The Egyptian lyre and the Celtic harp are tuned to a LA comprising 432 frequencies (which corresponds, of course, to the Pythagorian scale).

Knowledge has been lost and must be rediscovered. Originally, long before Pythagoras' time, the scale was calculated in relation to the position of the seven planets in the solar system. All the music of the spheres is founded upon this precept. All the divine and sacred numbers of the initiatory traditions on earth are founded on this reality, which vibrates to the rhythm of the planets. Since 1953, man is no longer "in tune" with the laws of the Universe! A dangerous error which threathens the equilibrium of the macrocosm-microcosm. Since 1953, all musical frequencies broadcast twenty-four hours a day around the world are "out of tune" with cosmic vibratory rhythms. How is it then possible to be surprised by the fact that the earth seems to be drying out and that the advent of the age of consciousness has been slowed down? One of the gravest responsibilities of the new composers of the Aquarian Ages is to retune their instruments to the universal frequency. Obviously, all cosmic rhythms and numbers are intimately linked to one another. The total of the figures in each is always 9 (3 $\times$ 3) or a multiple of 9: 54 (half of the Vedic and Tibetan 108), 72 (the Pythagorian sacred number), 234 (the symmetrical axial number of 432), 432 (the sacred number of the Druids or bardic LA), 504 (sacred number of southern Asia – 432 + 72), 666 (sacred number of the Book of Revelation). Bodily frequencies vibrate in harmony with cosmic frequencies. The physical body vibrates *with* the galactic body.

The heart beats at a rate of 72 times per minute. The sun takes 72 years (7 + 2 = 9) to travel through one degree in the zodiac. The moon's vibratory frequency is 216 (72 $\times$ 3). Everything is linked, always.

Can we reasonably think, or hope, that an energetic musical vibration that is out of tune with the cosmic could have, on a long term basis, a reharmonizing and beneficial effect? Music which does not hold sacred the laws of life cannot be as effective as a harmonic sound wave faithful to the dance of the Universe.

129

The reharmonization of the centres of consciousness through sound and colour

The "majority" school of medicine recognizes only one body: the physical body. We must admit that this perception reaches the limits of all that is restrictive, primitive and out-of-date. For millenia, human beings who have succeeded in elevating themselves beyond physical feelings by accelerating their molecular vibrations have recognized, through experience, the existence of an immaterial body, more subtle than the bodily envelope. Because it does not consist of physical atoms, this subtle or astral body cannot be perceived by the body's senses. For this reason, the humanoïd who has not gone through the process of purification aimed at developing clairvoyance, clairaudience, telepathy, intuition and the psychic powers in general, is doomed to remain in the limited space of his physical vision and hearing.

How many men and women, well-educated, university graduates, sure of themselves and of the paltry education they have received, thus completely bypass their freedom and happiness!

Genuine security, real health rests on one thing only: the harmonization of the subtle body. It is only when the body vibrates in sympathy with cosmic equilibrium that all physical life thrives. The appearance of the physical body is the direct reflection of the state of the subtle body. The anatomy of the subtle body has been known since time immemorial and the *Vedic Scriptures* explain it in detail. Ancient Chinese literature has also bequeathed important information on the topic. Thus, we know that this body is covered with minute specific points, which the Chinese called "*hsié*", corresponding to the points used in acupuncture. By activating them, it is possible to free crucial energy currents related to the proper functioning of the entire organism. Certain points are remarkable: they are the centres of energy, called *chakras* in Sanskrit. The word *chakra* means wheel of energy-consciousness. *Nadis*, a system of subtle nerves, link these centres to one another; clairvoyance shows these *chakras* under the form of spirals strangely resembling the black holes in space. The chakras are extremely powerful transmitter-receivers. If they are unbalanced or out of tune, all the emotional functions of the individual are affected. The manner in which existence is perceived directly depends on whether or not they are properly harmonized.

All sorts of tensions and fears usually block these centres and this accumulation of negative emotions prevents us from the full enjoyment of life's heritage which is, according to divine law, an inexhaustible treasure of serenity and abundance **at all levels**.

As nothing in the galaxy is left to chance, it is possible to exercise an immediate action on the *chakras*. Each of them reverberates "with" a particular frequency and corresponds to specific plains of consciousness. When these points are aligned and vibrate in harmony, the feeling experienced goes beyond human language. The most accurate words to express this feeling of plenitude are strength, health, beauty, knowledge, success in existence, living light and pure love. These centres of consciousness are seven in number and their counterparts in the various plains, visible and invisible, moveable and immoveable, are unlimited.

1- The consciousness-centre of Earth
(*muladhara chakra*)

This is literally the support, the basis of the incarnated being. Located at the perineum (between the anus and the genitals), it constitutes the floor of the individual. This centre links us to Mother-Earth and to all living entities inhabiting it. All our existential fears reside here. The root-centre can easily be cleansed from these useless and dangerous tensions by the colour **red**, the note **C** and the *bija-mantra* **Lam**, by letting the mental processes be peacefully absorbed by the corresponding positive assertions:
— I feel perfectly linked to Earth and to all beings on it. I love them and they love me. I thus have nothing to fear from them nor them from me. All is well.

Through visualization, I let the colour red and the sound vibration *Lammmm*... dissolve my fears. If something particularly frightens me, I allow myself to think about it, to visualize it and to admit that it really frightens me. I then let the colour red and the Lam sound transform this fear into cosmic dust. Tensions ease. I feel integrated into Earth and related to the beings upon it. Nothing exists in the universe that can frighten me. I feel perfectly protected and supported. The omnipresent forces of good, love me and protect me. I am the immortal soul, unalterable and eternally happy.

2- The consciousness-centre of water
(*svadhisthana chakra*)

This is the magical tree, the totem, the innermost seat of the being, his own individualization, his foundation. It is the *chakra* of sexuality and it is related to the water element. Creativity, freedom from sexual frustrations, blood circulation and social relations depend on its proper functioning. It reacts to the colour **orange**, to the note **D** and to the seed vibration **Vam**.

The assertions which correspond to it are the following:
— I visualize the colour orange and I sing the mantra *Vammmm...* on the note D. I feel that the synthesis of these frequencies cleanses and reactivates my reproductive organs. This action perfectly balances the masculine and feminine energies within me. Consequently, I am able to give and to receive; I am able to create everything that I can possibly conceive of. If I know that I bear within me a given residue, a complex, a sexual frustration, a specific trauma, I allow myself to think about it, to visualize it and to accept that it really exists, without trying to ignore it or to hide it. I then let the colour and the sound dissolve this tension and make it completely disappear.

I know that from now on, my sexual relations will be beautiful and free from fear, violence and egoïsm. I am able to create beautiful things. All my relationships are harmonious. I get along well with everyone. I have no more resentment towards anyone and no one is resentful towards me. I do not hold a grudge against anyone and no one does against me. The forces of good, love and protect me, everywhere and always. I am the immortal soul, indestructible, perfectly conscious and eternally happy. I am a part of God. I am divine. I am at one with God in quality. I am of divine essence.

3- The consciousness-centre of fire
(*manipura*)

In Sanskrit, *manipura* means "jewel-filled stronghold". This centre is located near the navel. It is genuinely filled with treasures since it is the seat of power, energy, personal feelings, purpose, free will and ambition. It is related to fire. It is the *chakra of the solar plexus, at the pit of the stomach. It controls anger and can be reactivated and rebalanced by the colour* **yellow**, the note **E** and the *bija-mantra* **Ram**.

The assertions which purify it are the following:
— I now use visualization of the colour yellow and the seed-sound *Rammmm...* sung on note E to act beneficially on my emotional consciousness. I use my inner power to balance my will and my feelings. I no longer take my brethrens' words and gestures as personal attacks. I know that there are no "bad people" in this world but only "suffering people". I forgive. If, in the past, I have been hurt by someone's words or gestures, I now choose to feel the hurt one last time and I admit that it exists. Then, I let it melt into the universe, carried by the vibrations of the colour yellow and by the sound *Ram*. I gradually feel the pain go away. I breathe the colour yellow and I am absorbed in the chant of *Ram*. The pain disappears and I feel stronger. I am the master of my emotions. I am the master of my will. I am aware of my own power. I am the immortal *atma*, indestructible and eternally happy. I am of divine essence. I am one with God in quality.

4- The consciousness-centre of air
(*anahata chakra*)

This is the heart's lotus. In Sanskrit, *an-ahata* means a sound created without being generated by physical action. Like a musical instrument that is not blown, not beaten, not strummed. This electromagnetic centre is linked to the soul. It is through this *chakra* that love is felt. It corresponds to the energetic centre of love. If we direct this love towards the inferior *chakras*, we "fall" in love and when these centres are unbalanced, love is tainted with egoïsm, possession and jealousy, blocking the elevation of the soul. If, on the contrary,

133

we direct it towards the higher *chakras*, we "rise" in love and chances are that this feeling will become beneficial, particularly if it is devoid of judgement and guilt, if it is directed towards unlimited states of consciousness.

The *chakra* of the heart harmonizes with the colour **green**, the note **F** and the seed-sound **Yam**. Upset, it provokes asthma, cardiac disorders, hypertension, etc...

Stones such as pink quartz, tourmaline and emeralds are particularly favourable to it. It corresponds to the air and is influenced by the planet Venus. The metal it is most sensitive to is copper. During reharmonization of this *chakra*, it is good to burn lavender or jasmine because these herbs vibrate in perfect harmony with the energies it holds within it.

Assertions for the centre of the heart are:

— I breathe the colour green and I chant the sound *Yammm...* on the note F. I feel that these vibrations strengthen my immune system. I now realize that I feel love for all types of people, independently from their condition, race, situation or exterior appearance. I feel that I genuinely love them. I feel grateful for all of humanity. The more I give, the more I receive. I feel that these vibrations and energies strengthen my whole body and brighten my mind. I feel that pure and unconditional love permeates my entire self. I feel my heart opening. I am capable of giving but also of receiving. I now visualize the person that I wish to love unconditionally. This relationship is my strength and my joy. I am the receptacle and the source of love. From my heart, a river of light shoots forth and irrigates the entire Earth. I am of divine essence, immortal. I am at one with God and I am at one with His love. I receive this love and spontaneously return it to all living beings.

5- The consciousness-centre of sound
(*visuddha*)

This is the centre of ether; only sound can penetrate ether and this is why the *visuddha chakra* is the transmitter-receiver of sound. Obviously, it is located just behind the throat and is directly related to the thyroid gland. When congested with negativity, the symptoms are easily identified: a sore throat, a stiff neck, a cold, ear problems and disorders of the thyroid gland. It is influenced by the planets Neptune and Mercury. Its activating stone is turquoise. This is the *chakra* of communication, expression, judgement. It expresses itself through the voice. Its colour is **blue**, its note **G** and its *bija-mantra* **Ham**.

Assertions freeing it from its blockages are:

— I visualize this person with whom I cannot fully communicate, (whether it is someone from my family, a friend or a business contact is of little importance). The energetic vibrations of the colour blue and the sound *Hammmm...* now help me to express what I feel. Moreover, I can express the slightest details of my life without keeping secrets. Thus, I feel how good it is to express myself. Words flow easily and I feel no tension. My throat opens, unknots itself and I feel that from now on, I am able to say everything I have always wished I could say.

I remember having been judgemental of my brethren. I hear again each word, each thought. I then feel the blue energy and the sound vibration *Ham* liberating me of all these judgements and words. I communicate my enthusiasm to others and I know everyone understands me. I am free to express everything I feel within. I am free of judgement and everyone understands my positive attitude. I am the free expression of God. I am the soul eternally free to communicate and express all the details of my divine life.

6- The consciousness-centre of light
(*ajna chakra*)

This is the third eye located on the forehead. In Sanskrit *ajna* means command. It is from this third eye that springs the thought-forms at the origin of all manifestations on the screen of our life. The human being is thus endowed with the most extraordinary instrument of creation. He can visualize what he desires and this image will manifest itself in his existence. There is no vision without light. It is through this centre that we possess the divine power to obtain **everything we choose** to imagine, consciously or unconsciously. If we can imagine something, we can obtain and reach it. Through *ajna chakra* everything we wish for ourselves or for our brothers is realized. Through *ajna chakra*, we are the command, the authority giving its orders to the circumstances of life. By directing this centre, we genuinely become masters. We are no longer meek victims resigned in the face of the events of existence.

The colour of this *chakra* is **indigo** (dark blue with red or violet undertones); its note is **A** and its *bija-mantra* **Om**. It influences the pineal gland. Its improper functioning provokes blindness, headaches, nightmares. It is influenced by the planet Jupiter and its metal is silver. The stone related to the third eye is quartz crystal.

The assertions influencing this *chakra* are:

— I now concentrate on something I truly desire. It could be something material or spiritual. I visualize this thing in the colour indigo, making it vibrate to the sound *Ommmm...* on the note A. I imagine this object, this situation or this circumstance in its every detail. I touch it through creative imagination, I feel its very surface, I breathe its perfume, I appreciate its exact forms with the help of my subtle vision; I hear its sounds. **Now, I project this vision into the world**. I feel that this image becomes reality in all its splendour and I am overwhelmed with joy. I know that everything I can dream of or imagine becomes a reality.

I visualize what I genuinely want to do with my life, with my destiny. I visualize my dearest desire in all its details, aromas, forms, colours, sounds, etc... and I project it into the world. I am the creator of my circumstances. No one else but myself is responsible for the events marking my existence. Everything I conceive becomes reality. I am of divine essence. I am at one with God in quality.

7- The consciousness-centre of beyond
(sahasrara chakra)

This *chakra* also has another name: *brahmarandra. Randra means opening. This passage gives us access to Brahman*, the spiritual plain. It is the door to heaven, located just above the head on the subtle body. It opens onto the realm beyond time and space. Its colour is **violet**, the last in the solar spectrum. It vibrates to the note **B** and its *bija-mantra* consists of all the sound frequencies connected with the Divine Names; these Names culminate in the *Maha-Vakya* or *Maha-Mantra* **A.U.M.** which is the complete representation of the Divine Father-Mother and everything that is.

This magnetic centre is related to the pituitary gland. When it is congested, the physical body and the mental react by depression, madness, boredom, the incapacity to face life. It is influenced by Uranus, its metal is gold and its beneficial stone is the diamond or even more so, the amethyst.

Its reactivating assertions are the following:
— I now visualize the God-Source as I conceive Him. This image is held above my head, bathed in the colour violet. I feel that this divine image enters into me and I integrate it. I let the three sacred letters A.U.M. make all the elements of my being vibrate.

A is the Father. U is the Divine Mother, M, all living creatures and all that is. Now, I visualize the God-Source and all that is and let the visualization carry me beyond my own understanding. Further and further, closer and closer. God is omnipresent. I let the divine image carry me where it wishes, in the exterior as well as the interior. In form as well as in non-form. The omnipresence becomes presence. This presence is within me. It is a part of myself and I am a part of it. It illuminates each of my *chakras*. All colours, all sounds become one. I feel I can really rely on this Presence. It is within me. It is real. It is everywhere in my life; It loves me. I know that this love relationship is infinite and absolute. I am perfectly loved. I am the immortal soul, eternally happy.

This reharmonization exercise of the astral body can be practised every day. In the morning to "charge" oneself with good frequencies and at night to "connect" with the Cosmic Energies in order to regain physical and subtle strength. Like Master Hermes, let us not forget **that everything is vibration, nothing is inert, everything vibrates, everything is balanced by compensating oscillations**; all cause has an effect, all effect has a cause, everything has a masculine and feminine principle, everything has two poles, everything is spirit. The human body is a sound box, a musical instrument which, like any other instrument, should be regularly tuned. Such a technical "tuning" ensures that we know a state of health, peace and unforgettable joy.

CHAPTER 4

THE INITIATORY EMOTION
OF THE SACRED NAMES

"The Eternal is one but has many names."

Rig Veda

"The experience of God is a flow, a totality, the infinite kalei-
doscope of life and death, the ultimate cause, the basis of
humankind, what Alan Watts called "the silence providing
all sounds". God is the conscience manifesting under the form
of a "lilac", the "game of the universe". God is the unut-
terable organizational matrix animating matter but that we can
know through experience."

Marilyn Ferguson
The Aquarian Conspiracy

"The basic knowledge enclosed in the mantra is not accessible
to thought, but sooner or later will return to be shared in a
spiritual manner by He who spiritually pronounces it within
himself, even though the word-to-word relationships remain
in themselves an enigma... Do not be unduly preoccupied by
the few Sanskrit words introduced into the text!"

Bô-Yin-Râ
The Practice of Mantras

"The clock cannot exist without the clock-maker."

Voltaire

139

The contemplative sound

The Sanskrit word *mantra* means "mental liberation". This sound or combination of sounds delivers the mental from its material conditioning and limits. Mantras are found in all cultures, traditions and religious systems. They are not exclusive to the Eastern world. Certain litanies from original Christianity are also mantras. Moslems, Buddhists and Zoroastrians also have their own specific mantras.

In our society, inspired by Judeo-Christianity, many people feel more in harmony with Christian mantric formulae, more closely related to their culture. This is encouraged. The mantra itself matters little provided we reach the ecstasy of spiritual deliverance, a mystical ecstasy that the sound vibration will undoubtedly trigger from the depths of any serious practitioner. Holy souls who have followed the path of authentic Christianity (from within the Catholic Church or from outside it, since belonging to a particular religious group is of no real importance) have reached the highest summits of unworldliness and of indestructible inner joy through the famous "prayer of the heart" or other effective incantations. In the revealed writings of this very same tradition, saints have found the path to salvation through contemplative sound.

On this topic, *The Accounts of a Russian Pilgrim* (author unknown) quotes Pierre Damascène's text, part of the illustrious *Philocaly*:

> "It is good to train oneself to invoke the Name of the Lord, more than to train the breathing, at all times, in all places, on all occasions. The adept says: "Pray incessantly. In this, he teaches that it is necessary to remember the Inner God at all times, in all places and in all things. If you make

something, you should think of the maker of all things that exist. If you see the light, remember He who has given it to you. If you consider the sky, the Earth, the sea and all things they contain, admire and glorify He who has created them. If you cover yourself with a garment, think of He who has given it to you and thank the Provider of your existence. In brief, may all gestures be a cause to celebrate the Creator; thus, you will pray incessantly and your soul will always be happy."

See how this process is simple, easy, and accessible to all those who have the slightest human emotion.

The thought expressed in the *Vedic Scriptures* is in absolute agreement with that of the *Philocaly*, when Chapter 9, Verse 27 of the *Bhagavad-Gita says*:

> *yat karosi yad asnasi yaj juhosi dadasi yat*
> *yat tapasyasi kaunteya tat kurusva mad arpanam*

"Whatever you do, eat, sacrifice and give, whatever austerity you practise, let it be an offering to Me."

The silent song of creatures

The Soufy tradition also accords great importance to the contemplation of the divine principle through listening to mystical sounds. According to the Koran (*Sourate* 17.44), every creature is in a constant state of prayer. The great commentator Purjavadi says that this song of praise consists of a harmony which the Ancient of All Days has placed within each entity. In a work entitled *Music and Ecstasy* (Musique et extase), exploring the vast field of the mystical and ecstatic musics of the Moslem world, expert Jean During explains that according to tradition:

"The silent song of creatures can be perceived by sages of enlightened heart, as was the harmony of the spheres. Abdulkarim Jili refers to a degree of enlightenment where the divine is revealed through the being's attributes as a listener. To some, God reveals Himself through the quality of hearing."

The Soufy practises the *dhirkr*, a technique of verbal memorizing, a kind of repetitive litany able to provide the *dhawq*, or taste, that is to say a direct experience. It is this taste, this feeling, this immense pleasure which is the God-Source's answer, a mystical pleasure offered in response to the contemplative sound. For the initiate of mystical sound, the ecstatic feeling which captivates him during musical hearing (*sama*), comes from luminous visions which appear and disappear. These visions are also fleeting intuitive states, but neverthelesss they are unforgettable.

When these magnificent flashes of lightning cross the sky of his consciouness, the initiate is moved by such happiness that for him, all worries related to the material form are annihilated. He knows he will never forget those confidential moments during which the entity of his inner being was revealed. Faithfully following the instructions of his Master-Guide, he absorbs his thought in the inner esoterical incantation. The power of the prayer-song is such that it suddenly reveals a state, a universal knowledge which was buried in the singer's farthest depths.

By constant prayer sent towards the Supreme Intelligence, the practitioner and the listener alike experience subtle states which originate in the invisible world. These states do not come from the exterior because the realm of light is everywhere within. The sacred song, materially silent but audible to the liberated and serene ear, brings nothing to the heart that it does not already have; **it suddenly brings to the surface what was already there for all eternity.**

The shabda, a conscious energy of light

There are two precise functions to listening to the words of power. On one hand, it provokes a certain loosening, a relaxation and can even go further by favouring the elimination of toxic substances, the healing of body and mind. On the other hand, and this is undoubtedly its most important role, it leads us towards the appreciation of our intimate being and towards awareness of the *atma*, the solar soul within us.

The music of the words of power is a manifestation of the *shabda* or primordial sound. It is an energy endowed with creative and transformative powers. This energy comes from God and is God. **The *shabda* does not function through the intermediary of physical sound vibrations. It is an energy of conscious light.** However, we should not attribute too much importance to the manner in which mantras are pronounced. The sound components which make up their structure are of little importance in themselves. This explains why variations of the syllable *om* (*ung* in Tibetan, *ang* in Chinese, and *ong* in Japanese; and even the *amen* of the Judeo-Christian tradition) **produce the same mantric effect!**

The *shabda* is the inner sound, the non-material vibration endowed with the power of liberating the sleeping forces esconced within us since the dawn of time. We are all the heirs and holders of these subtle energies. Born of the universal consciousness, each being represents an individual divine particle, a "son of God" (*aham bija-pradah pita*, Gita 14.4).

Whether the divine spark is at a point in its evolution where it must inhabit a carnal vehicle belonging to the vegetal, animal, human, angelic or devic reign is of no effect on its position (although an entity which has acquired a female body is often more intuitive than one which has acquired a male body; it should be noted that according to the *Vedic Scriptures*, from all points of view, man and woman are spiritually equal). Consequently, as part of the Great Whole and Absolute – sons and daughters of the perfect multiple unity – we have the power and the right to awaken our psychic forces and their corresponding *chakras* to the superior reality of the abstract absolute space. This awakening is induced by a sound vibration which is not material. Awakened by the *shabda* – the original inner sound – our subtle energies disentangle the centres of our etherial bodies and untie the electromagnetic points rendered sterile and inert because of an art of living in disagreement with the rhythm of life. Thus, the spiritual sound vibration – the mantra – makes the inner *shabda* vibrate in sympathy. And the *shabda* is the only force capable of healing illusion (maya) and capable of transmuting the lead of matter into the gold of the spirit.

The invisible reality

Scientifically, illusion would seem to be a holographic vision of the universe. Researcher Pribram had this vision. He believed that if the nature of reality is itself holographic, and if the brain functions holographically, then the world is actually a *maya*, or a temporary magical appearance and hence illusory before the permanence of reality. This amounts to saying that all the philosophies and ways of living born of rank materialism based on the sole reality of form and matter are the fruit of the furthest reaching deceit ever!

David Bohn – a disciple of Einstein – had arrived at a similar thought process. He described a holographic universe in some of his most important articles, calling for a new order in physics. In his opinion, what appears to be a stable, tangible, visible and audible world is an illusion. If matter is dynamic, ephemeral, kaleidoscopic, in perpetual movement, it cannot be real.

In fact, the world is real, but it is transitory. Beyond this world of passage exists an underlying order, a matrix of a superior reality. The ephemeral aspect of matter as a discovery of advanced physics is again confirmed by the *Vedic Scriptures* (Gita 8.20):

paras tasmat tu bhavo nyo
'vyakto' vyaktat sanatanah
yah sa sarvesu bhutesu
nasyatsu na vinasyati

"Incessantly, day after day, the day breaks, and each time myriads of entities are brought back to existence. Incessantly, night after night, the night falls and with it comes their annihilation, about which they can do nothing. However, another world exists, eternal, beyond the two states of matter, manifested and non-manifested. The Supreme World, which never perishes; when everything in the Universe is dissolved, it remains intact."

The *shabda's* non-material sound which designates the absolute consciousness holds the power to bring the conditioned being into the very midst of this invisible reality, which exists permanently beyond the physical, mental and intellectual sensory perceptions.

A unique ecological experience

The sound holds the key to the mysteries of life and creation and the maintenance of the universe. Sound vibration is also perceived as the best way to free oneself from material conditioning and slavery. Throughout the ages, philosophers have shown how the living entity is in a state resembling sleep. The best way to awaken someone is to call his name until he comes out of his sleep. In this context, the analogy of the sleeper awakened by the sound of his name is an accurate one, since the individual who is bewitched and poisoned by the soporific of the impermanent can be awakened to the eternal reality of "transcendental" resonances. The latter can be heard by listening to and chanting the sacred injunctions (*shabda-brahma*) or any other revealed Scriptures, such as the *Chilam-Balam*, the "Book of Books", the sacred jewel of pre-Colombian peoples. These activities are able to make the living being's inner *shabda* vibrate and are able to free him from the blockages restricting him to the confines of the physical world.

srnvatam sva-kathah krsna punya-sravana-kirtanah

> "The Infinitely Fascinating is in the heart of each being under the form of the supreme soul; the heart which develops the vivid desire to hear His message, He purifies from all physical desire." (*Srinad Bhagavatam* 1.2.17)

The transcendental sound, the message of the essential being contained in the *shabda-brahma* is in no way different from universal truth. Thus, each time one listens or conveys this sound vibration, the soul of the inner God manifests Its personal presence under the form of a sound holding all its power. This power alone is able to purify the intimate being from all its impediments.

The state of well-being that inevitably follows represents a unique experience, unforgettable and profoundly initiatory.

This purifying *shabda-brahma* is found in all great revelations aimed at awakening and elevating the human soul.

Whether these beneficial revelations originate from Eastern, Western, Lemurian, Egyptian or Atlantean civilizations is genuinely unimportant. What matters is the knowledge they carry; universal, practical and useful knowledge concerning the complete, uncompromising healing of environmental and psychological wounds caused by the planetary mistakes of those who pursue material exploitation at all costs.

It is necessary and urgent that the unique experience of spiritual sound vibration be experienced everywhere in the world because this experience triggers a profound change in the hearts of individuals. Through this process, barbarian and backward man gradually develops his human being's consciousness and renews contact with the living entity he bears within him – Mother-Earth. He then regains the awareness of being irremediably linked to oceans, forests, rivers, mountains and plains. He understands that each injury inflicted upon the Earth is unmistakably tatooed on his soul and body with the ink of war, famine and ecological catastrophes. From then on, he becomes a solar adult and ceases to bemoan his fate, putting an end to his self-destruction.

Healing through the sun-mantra

All the mantric forces represent an appeal. In other words, these sound formulae are used to obtain something. Sometimes, sounds act directly on matter; at other times, the mantra is addressed to the Divinity-Force which presides over a particular physical element. The *om ghrami suryay namah* mantra, for instance, is sung when a serious illness appears. It is practised while the sun is half risen. The patient stands facing the sun's rays, holding in his right hand a copper pot filled with pure water. He then offers the water to the sun and chants the mantra three times. Afterwards, it is recommended that the mantra be sung as often as one wishes, until the patient is cured.

This purification ritual is mentioned in a very ancient book entitled "*Aditya Hriday*", given in Sanskrit by Krishna to Samb, one of his sons, who at the time was suffering from an incurable illness. After a while, Samb was cured. The story of this very special mantra was recounted to me by the famous Ramesh Chandra Jyotishi, also known under the name of Mauna Baba, an astrologist from Vrindavan (India).

There are mantras suited to all needs. Some bring wealth, others, protection; others still bring health. The list is infinite and there are as many mantric possibilities as there are desires in the human heart. However, we will see that the most liberating mantras are those diametrically opposed to the requests of the "ego". These are mantras which do not represent requests but which, passed down from one disciple to the next, are formed by the Inner God's revealed Names, under the multiple aspects of the Absolute Being, sung in an altogether spontaneous manner.

A pure light of love

Of all known mantras, the "mantras of the Names" are the most powerful since they are surrounded with the halo of the pure light of love and the soul which sings them expects nothing in return. Reciting them is a gratuitous, devotional act. The song of the Names is not the result of a particular calculation, of "trade" with the divine forces. These mantras correspond to a spontaneous feeling which springs from the depths of the heart.

All great thinkers of visualization and creative assertion are unanimous in saying that the spoken word is that much more powerful when it is pronounced not in a state of mind implying a lack of, an imploring or a request but rather as thanks or acknowledgment, knowing that we have already received.

A song of joy of inconceivable power

To wish or appeal for health, for example, proves to the subconscious that the body does not possess it and that consequently it lacks it. In no way can a lack create a fulfilment. **One lack inevitably**

results in a greater lack. Like success leads to success, the feeling of emptiness or lack of something actually provokes a state of emptiness. Similarly, the vibrating waves irradiating from a feeling of fright inevitably lead to the events at the origin of such a feeling. Fearing something is the best way to ensure that the dreaded event takes place. **Feeling the reality of a set of circumstances unfailingly results in that reality.**

Thus, the true positive and creative assertion is not a request or a question but a response corresponding to a feeling of plenitude.

In the practice of the Sacred Names, the same law applies. This is why the song of the Name is not a prayer, since a prayer most often involves a petition. One claims the satisfaction of a desire or implores something. In opposition to this state of solicitation, the mantra of the Name is free. Without supplication, it provides limitless joy, inexpressable in human language. The soul which practises such a song – regardless of the particular Name it feels attracted to, and if such is the case, regardless of the system of thought it draws inspiration from – does not demand anything, does not implore, does not beg, does not solicit. From its lips comes a song of joy which does not command nor give orders. The only desire remains the desire to stay in the ecstatic presence of the Name, for the vibration of the living light is absolutely no different from His Name. Because of this non-differentiation which renders them inseparable from the absolute, the Sacred Names hold inconceivable spiritual powers.

A state of non-differentiation

At the physical level and in a material sense, the name is different from the form. In fact, language – whose function it is to express thought and serve as a communications link between men – is simply a symbolic representation. Vocal and graphic signs represent a given object or person but do not incarnate the reality they seek to evoke, imitate or replace. We have seen that they serve in building "bridges" of harmonic resonance between the person who pronounces them and the objects or beings they represent. We could say that they are the ambassadors of reality, but they are only its symbols. The word "water" is not the element water; it only links us harmonically to water.

On the contrary, in the field of Sacred Names, the symbol incarnates the reality. This is why according to Vedic thought, the Divine Name is the sound incarnation of the divine principle. Precious information is found on its sovereign effectiveness in all Holy Scriptures such as the Bible, the Koran, the Torah, etc. But it is probably in the *Vedic Scriptures* that references to multiple Absolute frequencies are the most numerous and the most precise.

Thus, the manner in which they manifest a unique energy in their state of non-differentiation is explained in the *Padma Purana*:

> "The Holy Names provide limitless joy to the souls who sing them. They grant all spiritual blessings, because they are God Himself, the cosmic reservoir of ultimate pleasure. These Names are complete in themselves and represent the perfect form of all peace and of all transcendental maturity. They do not correspond to a material sound or name under any condition whatsoever, and they are no less powerful than the Source of all cosmic energies. Unsoiled by material vibrations, they are never involved in the games of illusion. Free and absolute, they are never conditioned by the laws of physical nature."

Sounds from another world

The famous Vaishnava poet of the seventeenth century, Narottam, who practised the song of the Name, wrote:

golokera prema-dhana hari-nama sankirtana

> "Transcendental sound vibrations have no other origin than the world of non-matter, the spiritual realm."

Two hundred years before, the avatar Chaitanya sang in the verses of his "*Shikshastak*":

> "O Sublime Intelligence, Your innumerable Names are vested with all good fortune for the universe's living entities. Of names, You have an unlimited

number and through them, You expand into the infinite. Moreover, each of these Names is charged with a specific and all-powerful energy.''

Therefore, the different sound frequencies used to name the cosmic reality are not composed of ordinary syllables or sounds. These sounds originate in the other world, a world located beyond the material atmosphere. However, the divine nature of the Sacred Name remains a total mystery for the soul which approaches it only through the means of logic and intellectual reasoning. Only the entity for whom it is possible to surpass all concepts and all prejudice, who involves himself directly in the practice of the song in a humble state of mind, without disdain nor pride, but with trust and love, will understand and fully enjoy the ecstasy of the supreme sound. Invisible radio waves travel from one place to another and can be heard when an electronic receiver catches them. In the same manner, spiritual waves can be perceived and assimilated by the entity equipped with the qualities required to receive them: a conscience in peace and a heart open to pure love. Furthermore, the feeling of a need for freedom and **the taste for experiment** will be precious assets to the person who chooses to follow this path.

At the instant of leaving the body

The Bible of Christians, the Koran of Moslems, the Torah of Hebrews, the Vedic Scriptures of Hindus and all books serving to enlighten humankind are unanimous on one major point: the divine principle – regardless of its Name, Aspect or the Actions attributed to Him – is the source of all entities. Therefore, the living being is a sub-product of an all-powerful seed, regardless of the culture, tradition, religion or region of the world he identifies himself with in this present life. In addition, this sub-product possesses the same qualitative potential as its creator. The Master Jesus has asserted this truth for 2,000 years:

"Be perfect as your Heavenly Father is perfect."
(*The Gospel* according to Saint Matthew – 5:48)

151

The *Vedic Scriptures* clearly teach that the living being is at one and the same time, at one with the universal Father, and simultaneously different from Him (*achintya – bhedabheda – tattva*). As a part and particle of the complete and absolute Whole, the divine spiritual spark possesses its qualities. Eternity (*sat*), consciousness (*chit*) and happiness (*ananda*) are therefore the supra-natural heritage of all entities. The sole difference between the Cosmic Soul and the infinitesimal spark is quantitative, although at the level of the absolute, all is essence.

From time immemorial, the entity has chosen to experience all sorts of situations with the goal of directing and controlling creation as he wishes and as he pleases. This is why he clothes himself in a physical body, which serves him as a vehicle for a few earthly years. After a while, this ephemeral body returns to the elements and consequently, the living being leaves it to reinstate a new body; the forms and qualities of this new vehicle of flesh are determined by the activities, desires and memories gathered in the course of the soul's life in the previous body. On this topic, the second section of the *Baghavad-Gita*, this unique text which André Malraux describes as composed of divine words, is once again very clear:

> "At the instant of death, the soul takes on a new body as naturally as it has passed, in the previous one, from childhood to youth and then to old age. This change does not trouble the one who is aware of his true nature. Know that what penetrates the whole body cannot be destroyed. No one can destroy the unperishable soul. Only the bodies it borrows are subject to destruction. The soul does not die with the body. Living, it will never cease to be. At the instant of death it clothes itself with a new body, as easily as one throws away old garments to put on new ones, since the other body is now useless." (*Bhagavad-Gita* 2.13.22)

In Section 8, Verse 6 of the same text, we find the following fundamental information:

yam yam vapi smaram bhavam
tyajaty ante Kalevaram
tam tam evaity Kauneteya
sada tad bhava-bhavitah

"The human being's thoughts and memories at the instant of leaving the body determine his future condition."

It is therefore possible to modify one's condition at the critical moment of physical death. The question is knowing how to leave the body or "die" in the desired mental condition. Our thoughts at the moment of death are mainly determined by the sum of our actions and thoughts over the course of our entire life. These actions and thoughts are themselves determined by singing and listening to words, music and all the sound waves which constantly permeate our subconscious. **The sound vibrations perceived in the present determine our future condition!** Thus, spiritually absorbed in the inner enlightenment acquired by listening to the Sacred Names and Pure Universal Music, in the course of our life, we will be able to acquire, while leaving our actual bodily envelope, a spiritual and eternal body, conscious of and happy in a different molecular structure.

Listening to the sacred sound vibrations linked to the Divine Names is thus the simplest means of reaching a superior plain of existence.

The worst of errors

Hypnotized and narrowly conditioned by matter's atmosphere, the living being is literally submerged in a world of dreams and illusions which are never the fruit of so-called luck, but quite the contrary, which are mainly his own inclinations, thoughts and memories. For the living being, this hypnotic condition of death and rebirth (*samsara*) corresponds on one hand to the oblivion of the original source – and on the other hand, to a state of chronic torpor into which the soul has gradually fallen while losing, from one rebirth to the next, the awareness of its inherent serenity, of its constitutional eternity and of its prodigious celestial origin. This state of torpor, comparable to a deep sleep, is at the origin of the tragedy of materialistic civilizations and empires which, through sheer ignorance of reality, base their knowledge on imperfect sensory observation, their monetary equilibrium on a totally inconsequential interpretetion of Earth's wealth, and their happiness on a laborious, ungrateful and dangerous stimulation of the senses.

This way of life is very risky. Indeed, under the laws governing the universe, these societies can never lay the blame on extenuating circumstances and they are irremediably swept away on the waves of time. Thus, regularly, atheist civilizations, **that is to say, civilizations in discord with the fundamental harmonics of the universe**, disappear from the face of the Earth, so far removed are they from the genuine values of existence. The fall and destruction of great materialistic empires, which unfortunately mark the history of the world, correspond to the deep sleep of the conditioned soul which painfully persists in searching for life on paths leading only to death.

Wanting to acquire happiness by engaging in activities which only aim at satisfying mental and sensual needs is the worst of errors for the soul. It is urgent to understand that the world can only survive by awakening to the truth of the soul. Any other consideration, whether economical or political, will only be of minor interest and will draw the planet even further into obscurantism, war, savagery and finally, annihilation.

Waking up the one who sleeps

Consider a fish out of water, no object, no situation can fully satisfy it. The only thing that could content it would be to return to its element: water. Similarly, nothing is better suited to perfectly satisfying the human being than the spiritual sound vibration which is actually his eternal element. The individual soul is a particle of the universal soul; its cosmic position consists in living, loving and working spontaneously in harmony with the galaxy as a whole. But it is prevented from doing so by the state of chronic sleep in which it has foundered. Therefore, each of us has the mission of awakening within himself this marvellous spark which has lain dormant for so long. Such is the true goal of our human lives, before dreams and illusions carry us towards even more difficult conditions of existence.

154

It is universally recognized that sound has the power to draw the consciousness out of sleep, to awaken it. Who has not experienced the ringing of an alarm clock? Along the same lines, the soul asleep in the bed of the physical world can awaken to real life through spiritual sound vibration. The latter is mainly present in the sound of the Sacred Names designating the essential cosmic principle. It is buried there, hidden away, and one of the means of perceiving it is to seek it through the practice of listening and singing these fabulous Names.

Chaitanya taught 500 years ago:

Namnam akari bahu-dha nija-sarva-saktis

"The sound vibration of Your Name can alone, O Lord, overwhelm the soul with all graces. Of sublime names, You possess an infinite number, vested with all spiritual powers; to sing them, no strict rule exists."

The great reality of inner sound

It is not new. Thousands of years ago, the illustrious Gitopanishad mentioned the sacred nature of the singing of and listening to the Divine Names:

"Among the sound vibrations, I am om, the absolute syllable, and among the means to spiritual realization, I am the japa, the song of Sacred Names."

(*Gita* 10-25)

The Bible itself teaches:

"Whoever invokes the Name of the Lord will be saved".

(Acts)

The Psalms describe the means by which the soul is liberated from material contingencies:

"May the sons of Sion praise the name of Yahweh through dance and song."

This divine sound vibration which holds the power to awaken the sleeping soul is the eternal *shabda-brahma*. Originally, the *shabda-brahma* was composed of names, acts, attributes and qualities of the highest reality. *Shabda* is, as we have seen, the original inner sound. It is this non-material vibration which enjoys the power to liberate the sleeping forces esconced within us since the dawn of time. We are all the heirs and holders of these subtle energies. The awakening of these energies can be manifested by means of this magical force. Thus awakened, our subtle energies disentangle the centres of our etherial bodies and unknot the electromagnetic points rendered sterile and inert because by an art of living in opposition with the universe's rhythm. The spiritual sound vibration makes the self's whole interior vibrate harmoniously and this unique force is capable of healing the illnesses inherent in the realm of illusion.

A song filled with peace

"It will be necessary for the human being to learn how to use sound if he wishes to participate in any way in the divine work. The first magical manifestation will then be the incantation. The priest – of whatever religious persuasion – will be the priest "accurate of voice" of Egyptian tradition, or the Indian singer, or the solar hero of mythology, the great Hermes whose song attracted to him animals drunk with joy."

Thus writes Anne Osmont in her book entitled *Rhythm, Creator of Forces and Forms* (Le rythme, créateur de forces et de formes).

One of the most beautiful fruit of the music of the soul consists in appeasing fear and anger. Regardless of our cultural or ideological belonging, our "song" – when it rings out well and genuinely – holds the mysterious power to transform a wild animal into a being filled with love and gentleness. It is essential to realize that the strength we project in song, sound, the spoken word and in music enters, for the most part, into the realization of the divine work, since the latter depends upon the musical sound wave. The mode of expression and the singer's motivation are primordial to obtain a sensitive effect. Human and universal pacification is the sacred song in itself, **when**

it is held within the singer's intent. The sung formula can therefore set free all its strength, not merely touching exterior things, but also the inner rhythms of the material or celestial universe. At this level of understanding, sound becomes a vibration comparable to a type of magnetism acting on the secret nature of human beings much more effectively than on visible organs. Herein also lies the power of mantras. The incantatory chant, rhythmical and sung is "charged" with the intent of the individual who makes it vibrate. At this moment, it is irresistible.

The *Gandharva Veda*, the book of the celestial singer, is a veritable treatise on sacred song and magical music and a great number of its songs can lead the initiate to certain states of ecstasy. To express their power, history tells us that Ravana – the magician who kidnapped Sita from Rama but failed to seduce her since genuine love is a magic infinitely more resistant than all others – had incurred Shiva's anger with his audacity. Only one glance from Shiva was enough to reduce the presumptuous magician to dust. Ravana suddenly remembered the "song that appeases anger" and, having evoked this true song of the spheres, he introduced peace and unconditional love into the heart of the angered god, thus obtaining his forgiveness.

Sounds which charm tigers

It is enough to relax muscle tension, to breathe deeply and, while visualizing a peaceful image, to slowly repeat the word *Shanti* (peace), preceded and followed by the syllable **om**, to genuinely feel the most extraordinary of sensations: peace.

In the *Sri Chaitanya Charitamrita* of Krishnadas Kaviraj Goswami, we can read the story of the great saint Mahaprabhu who, like Hermes and the transformative power of his lyre, could charm wild animals with only the sound of his voice. The text relates that one day, Mahaprabhu was crossing the jungle of Kataka in Bengali, completely absorbed in the singing of the 32-syllable mantra (the mantra of ancient *Purana*, composed of the Holy Names Krishna, Rama

157

and Hare). Attracted by the sound of his voice, the many tigers haunting the jungle at the time surrounded him without hurting him in the least. When Balabhadra Bhattacharya – Mahaprabhu's companion – saw him touch one of the tigers with his foot, he was petrified with terror. But the tiger's attitude surprised him even more. The animal raised himself onto his back paws and began to roar in delight. It then began to dance to the rhythm of the mantra, bewitched by Mahaprabhu's soft voice.

In all civilizations and in all initiations, we find the assurance that sound – and in particular the absolute sound of the names designating the Divine Power – represents the most powerful of transformative energies known in creation.

God as sound

The preceding anecdote shows to what extent the 32-syllable mantra (also called *maha-mantra*, or great mantra) can be powerful. In fact, the ancient *Puranas* describe this mantra as being "God as sound", similar to the A.U.M. vibration. Therefore, it is not surprising that sung with a perfectly pure heart, it has the power to make wild animals dance. The chant of this mantra is so powerful that it can even penetrate the hearing of trees and plants! What could be said, then, of animals and human beings...

The story of master Haridasa tells that he had been asked how trees and plants could be freed from material contingency. Haridasa answered that singing the *maha-mantra* aloud is not only of invaluable help to beings conditioned by a form of plant life, it is also beneficial to insects and to all living beings. The special power of the *maha-mantra* comes from its celestial origin. This category of High Sound Vibrations has been brought to Earth regularly over the course of thousands of years by Entities from the invisible spheres.

It is also thus for the unlimited number of various audible revelations (such as Cristos, Allah, Buddha, Yaweh, Adonaïs, etc...) known on Earth. It is quite obvious that in other places in the universe, these sound frequencies are distinct from those known on Earth. These disparities are caused by the diversity of languages and by more or less true perceptions of divine realities. The celestial entity or the specially empowered messenger who manifests himself in a particular culture, transmits the spiritual sound vibration to an entity conditioned by the modes of matter. The latter entity is himself gradually purified and in turn transmits the audible revelation to other entities. This is called the system of inheritance of disciples or *parampara*. This system is capable of awakening the incommensurate energy of the primordial frequency in each of us. The only condition for freeing all its power is to listen to it, to chant it or to remember it with great purity of heart, with no motivation of a material order.

A multitude of names for a single essence

In a work entitled *Sri Chaitanya-Shikshamrita* (The Sublime Teachings of Sri Chaitanya), Srila Bhaktivinode Thakur – one of India's greatest philosophers – clearly explains why the superficial differences existing between the Sacred Names of the great religions are, in fact, of no importance whatsoever. According to Bhaktivinode, although human nature is the same everywhere, people living in different countries and on different continents acquire various secondary characteristics. **It is impossible to find in this world two peoples with the same secondary nature**. If we can observe different personalities and appearances in two brothers born of the same mother, then it is obviously natural to note a disparity between men born in different regions of the globe.

In the Earth's countries, phenomena such as the location of waterways, the movements of air masses, mountains, forests and the quantity of available foods and garments of all sorts, all show very marked variations. Consequently, certain differences naturally appear in physionomy, social positioning, activity, music, religion, styles of clothing and food preferences. Because each nationality has a particular way of viewing life, various conceptions of reality will seem to be superficially opposed, **but they are of the same essence**. What will seem to be opposed (without really being so) will be the name each nation, each people, will give to the universal divine principle.

Just as in different places people awaken from their primitive condition and gradually develop culture, science, laws and devotion for the universal substance, their adoration will also be divergent in vocabulary, customs, nature of offerings, music and inner attitude. However, if we consider all these apparent disparities from an impartial point of view, we will encounter no contradiction, no evil, as long as the object of adoration remains the same. It is therefore appropriate to execute in the purest of virtue our inspired meditative or mantric song, **without ever ridiculing the meditative codes of others**.

Why should a Christian make war with a Moslem? Why should a Buddhist judge a Hindu? All human beings are seekers in the immense cosmos and they sense the same Energy simultaneously and inconceivably, personally and impersonally at the same time. Therefore, they should unite their efforts, their testimonies and their research. In the light of the factors mentioned previously, systems which elevate consciousness and which are applied throughout the world present five major differences:

1) different spiritual masters
2) different emotional states linked to meditation
3) different rituals
4) different affections and activities with regard to the focus of concentration
5) different terminologies and appellations resulting from use of different languages.

In keeping with the variety of revealed guides and texts, in some regions men honor the sages of Vedic culture, in other places, they revere Mohammed and his prophets and in other regions still, they are attached to the holy individuals who follow the teachings of Jesus. Similarly, each locality shows a particular respect for different great philosophers. Each community should, of course, honour its own spiritual masters, guides or teachers, **but no one should try to prove the superiority of his master's instructions under the pretext of acquiring a great number of followers**. The propagation of such antagonistic positions would be disastrous! With regard to adoration, prescribed rituals vary according to the individual's devotional sentiments and mentality. In certain areas, the spiritualist sits in a place of power, practises renunciation and breath control. Elsewhere, he prostrates himself five times a day in the direction of his master's tomb in order to offer his praise without worry concerning the situation he is in. Yet elsewhere, he kneels in the temple or in his home, his hands joined, admits to being an indestructible soul and glorifies the divine principle.

Each type of adoration differs in clothing, food, cleanliness, etc... Moreover, the feeling and the conduct towards the adored Object vary from religion to religion. Certain devotees, their consciousness saturated with devotion, install a form of God in their hearts, in their thoughts or on an altar. Other processes, more inclined to logical reasoning, completely reject the external image; hence, the initiate must create a concept of the Ultimate Cause in his mind and must adore It. Nevertheless, we should realize that **all** Deities or "Objects", concrete, abstract, visible, or invisible, described in the various Scriptures, are in reality authentic representations of the Absolute.

Above all, it is important to grasp that different languages give the Absolute various names. Religious systems also have different names and they have given an appropriate appellation to each object of worship. Because of the five great differences previously mentioned, a great number of the world's religions have developed very differently from one another. **However, these differences should not be the source of mutual disagreements, since this would lead to real disaster**.

Truth is one

If, at the hour of prayer, we find ourselves in the temple of a religious group different from ours, we should think: "Here, the Absolute is worshipped in a new way; It is referred to by a Name different from the one I know. It is not obligatory that I participate in this ritual; however, this scene creates within me a more intense feeling for my own meditation. **Absolute truth is one**. Therefore, I offer my praise to the Form I see here and I pray the Infinite (from which this "Form" is born) that this particular Deity help me increase my love for Him."

Those who do not act in this way, but who show malice or envy or who ridicule other meditative processes, certainly deviate from true spirituality, thus proving their lack of universal vision. When these people will have truly elevated their vibratory frequencies through one process or another, they will no longer be attracted by this sort of useless quarrel. Pure love (*Prema*), in fact, incarnates the eternal religion of the spiritual soul (*sanatan-dharma*), and hence, in spite of the five great differences which distinguish the religions of the world, **we should recognize as truthful, all processes of purification and acceleration whose goal is attaining devotion for all aspects of the Divine Principle (*Bhakti*).**

It is useless to quarrel over a name or over puerile dissension. The value of a method of Self realization cannot only be "judged" by the purity of the goal it is aimed at reaching. Reading the thoughts of Bhaktivinode Thakur, one grasps all the futility, all the extreme ignorance and all the formidable hypocrisy which lead men to kill one another in the name of a particular God! We understand once and for all that so-called religious wars are, in fact, wars of power, wars of profit, led by the mere cupidity and the mere savagery of a few regressive people **disguised as religious people** and who, unfortunately, still find in our time unscrupulous people to follow them...

Attempting the experience of the Universal Name

It is not necessary to adopt an official religion to progress spiritually or to practise singing the Names of Power. It is possible that for certain people, for whom the term "revealed" means strictly nothing, it is impossible to find a resonance of any type in any Scriptures and the Latin word *religare* – (to link oneself with the Absolute) – remains enigmatic. For many, God is dead or is an abstraction, a dream, a utopia. Not having met an *acarya* (living master who only "preaches" through example) and followed by their family or immediate circle of friends and acquaintances, these people have not made the effort of seeking further and have simply accepted, **without personal investigation**, the materialistic ideas proposed by the majority. Without really knowing why, they have reached the conclusion that an omnipresent supra-natural power cannot exist in a world where war, obscurity and hatred are rampant.

An alien landing in the middle of a desert would not see any trace of water and could make the same kind of error by concluding that the element of water cannot exist on Earth. The calamities and misfortunes of creation do not necessarily imply the non-existence of a creator. **The happiness and misfortune of men is only the rightful reward of their words, actions, thoughts and music**.

Be this as it may, it is not a matter of believing or not, but rather of doing, of experiencing and "tasting". Whether or not the word God has a meaning for us, there is no reason for us to change our way of seeing things. The seeker who has not yet experienced the revelation of the Inner Presence can just as easily start the work of transformation with a simple supposition: the original cause thus becomes a work hypothesis. Is this not, after all, the most commonly employed method in pure science?... Whatever our convictions, it is always possible to choose a sound vibration composed of one of the known sacred frequencies and to use it to our own benefit. What is important is to sing the Name, regardless of what tradition it belongs to. To attempt the experiment of the experience of the name, it is not even necessary to believe in a Superior Intelligence or not.

Sit comfortably, a little out of the way, breathe deeply and relax. Let your mind wander without fighting it, as you would let the water flow in a river, and simply, naturally, experience the Name. **To listen is all that is necessary**. From the lips, the sound travels to the ear and descends into the heart. The activity of the senses and of the mental then seems to stop and one experiences a happiness that no language is able to describe. One feels peace and joy worthy of the beauty of life. One discovers the wonderful melody of genuine love and this primordial vibration has the power to liberate us from the cycle of deaths and rebirths by setting us on the road home, towards peace and light. It is as simple as that!

The immortal nectar

As we have seen, a mantra is a sound structure whose modulations hold a proven power. Often formed from the Sanskrit alphabet's fifty signs – the *dévanagari*, or language of the gods – the mantra allows the mental to come to know concentration. Most mantras used for meditation are chosen from among the multiple names designating the primary source. The repetition of such mantras is called *japa*. A great many masters have corroborated the Vedic science by emphasizing that the *japa* is especially recommended for our present age, as an effective means of reaching Self realization.

> Harer nama harer nama harer namaiva kevalam
> kalau nasty eva nasty eva gatir anytha

"In the age of Kali – which we are presently living through – the chanting of sacred names, the japa, represents the method, the true technique to reach enlightenment." (*Puranas*)

In fact, the *japa* is called *yuga-dharma*: the means of reaching salvation, the duty of every living being (*dharma*) in this particular great cosmic cycle, the *Kali Yuga*.

Chanting and listening (the famous *sravanam kirtanam*) is an easy method that can be practised at all ages. If we do not feel any particular attraction for one Sacred Name, or if we do have some prejudice in favour of one of the Sacred Names, we need only choose the one most suited to us. For instance, if the name Rama or Krishna (the Infinitely Fascinating and the Source of all pleasures) is disturbing to us for one reason or another, we can practise singing the name of Christ or Cristos (the light), or else Allah (Al: without a beginning; laah: without an end), or Jehovah, Yahwe, Adonaïs or Buddha (the Enlightened) etc...

Consequently, even though we are of a given religious persuasion, whether we consider ourselves to be Hindus, Christians, Buddhists or Moslems, we can easily commit ourselves to the practice of the Name as outlined in the spiritual message we are conditioned to accept by education, culture or tradition. It is essential to develop the memory of the inner divinity.

As it is possible to learn mathematics in any university, one can develop the love of God by following any given authentic path. Thus, the Name in itself matters little. What is important is to sing it or to listen to it. Singing and listening allow us to experience the very nature of the Name. We taste the immortal nectar. No word is worthy of describing this unforgettable experience. One can, for instance, write pages about the nature of honey, analyze the elements composing the substance, point out that honey is sweet, smooth and flavourful etc. But no explanation, no book nor any lecture will replace direct experience. It suffices to taste it to "know" it. Likewise, the transcendental nature, spiritual and absolute, of the Name cannot be known otherwise than by direct experimentation. It is not a question of believing, but of doing; not of judging, but of experimenting; not of speculating, but of acting.

There is no material barrier to the singing of the Name. A Moslem can sing the name of Allah; a Christian, that of Christ; a Hindu, that of Rama, Krishna or Narayan; a Buddhist, that of Buddha. Nor is it necessary to be rich or poor, learned or ignorant. It costs nothing: the song of the Name is free. It can be practised everywhere, under all circumstances, with anyone. Everyone can sing it and draw the greatest benefit from this universal practice. For this singing and listening, no strict rule exists. On many occasions, the singing of the Name is recommended in Biblical Scriptures. The Psalms urge us to sing and glorify it:

> "All nations that You have created will come before Thee, O Lord, and will glorify Thy Name."

The Chronicles also give us this precious advice:

> "Give thanks unto the Lord, call upon his name, make known his deeds among the people; sing unto him, sing psalms unto him, talk ye of all his wondrous works; glory ye in his holy name: let the heart of them rejoice that seek the Lord." (I *Chronicles* 16:8-10)

In the New Testament, Saint Paul says:

> "For there is no difference between the Jew and the Greek: for the same Lord over all is rich unto all that call upon him; for whosoever shall call upon the name of the Lord shall be saved." (*Romans* 10:12-13)

The great Master Jesus has the same message:

> "I have manifested thy name unto the men which thou gavest me out of the world: thine they were, and thou gavest them me; and they have kept thy word." (*John* 17:6, 11-12)

And thus he taught us to pray:

> " Our Father, hallowed be Thy Name."

Active meditation

Like the instrumentalist who each day practises scales and arpeggios, the composer, who wishes his music to be of the type that touches the highest and purest regions in the human being, or the simple initiate who wishes to attain well-being and the vision of the invisible, meditates daily on the essential realities of the universe. He regularly exercises his mental powers to the arpeggios of peace, beauty, truth and benevolence. His daily exercise is active meditation. His scales will be composed of the sounds designating the Infinite, according to the tradition which suits him, regardless, I must repeat, of whether it is of Eastern or Western origin. He can concentrate more specifically on the mantra received from his personal guide during initiation; but this practice does not prevent him from exercising his mind to the frequencies of the words of power proceeding from all the thought processes known on our planet or from those of other galaxies. Singing the Name has always been recognized as a means of authentic and effective realization. When one comes into contact with electricity, one feels its energy, regardless of the vector through which it has been transmitted.

The absolute sounds of various traditions:

Sacred Names according to Islam

"God is great"	Allahu Akbar
"There is no other God than God"	La Ilah Ill'Allahu
"In the name of Allah, the compassionate"	Bishmillah Ir-Rahman Ir-Rahim
"In the name of Allah"	Bishmillah
"God is great"	Allah, Allah

The prophet Mohammed had the habit of saying:

> "The hour of death will not take by surprise he who sings the Name of the Lord."

Sacred Names according to Christianity

"Lord Jesus Christ"
"Jesus, Jesus"
"Holy Mary, mother of God"
"Om Jesum Christum"

In the book entitled *The Wonders of the Holy Name*, we can read:

> "The name of Jesus is the shortest, easiest and most powerful of prayers. Everyone can say it, even while in the midst of his daily tasks. God cannot refuse to hear it."

Sacred Names according to Hinduism

"Om Namo Bhagavate Vasudevaya"
"Sri Ram, Jai Ram, Jai Jai Ram"
"Hare Krishna, Hare Krishna, Krishna Krishna, Hare Hare Hare Rama, Hare Rama, Rama Rama, Hare Hare" (*Maha-Mantra*)
"Hari Om"
"A.U.M."

Sacred Names according to Buddhism

"Namu Amida Buddhsu"   I offer my praise to Lord Buddha
"Kwanzeon Bosatsu"   O compassionnate Bodhisattva
"Om Mani Padme Hum"   O Thee, the Divine in me!

The *zendo*, a well-known Buddhist treatise, says the following on this topic:

> "Simply repeat the Name of Amida with all your heart, when you are lying down or seated, when you are walking or when standing still, never cease to practise the Name, even for one instant. Such is the work that infallibly provides salvation, as it is in concordance with Buddha's original desire."

> "The greatest medicine is the call of the Name of Amida (Buddha) and this call is contained in the six syllables NA MU A MI DA BU. This chant represents the perfect concentration on the Name of Buddha. To practise it, no knowledge is required. All we need do is pronounce the words and listen. In the sound of these six syllables lies the pivotal point of a fundamental power." (*Hakuin*, Zen Buddhist, 18th Century).

In the daily practice of chanting and listening to these various sound sequences, it is useless to persist in lending them a relative value. Divine Intelligence is present in all universes, and the Names attributed to Him, although different from one place to another, nonetheless are not opposed to His absolute nature.

Indeed, the Names designating the universal necessity are all vested with the same sacred character since they all indicate the same Absolute Person or the same Supreme Energy, depending on the case. These Sacred Names have a power identical to that of the Source-Being; nothing can thus be opposed to the fact that each of us, **in whichever part of the universe he resides in**, whether it be inside our solar system or in another galaxy, spontaneously sings and praises the Great Whole through the specific name which in a given area, serves to designate It. These Names, source of all good fortune, are not facilities of a material order. For them to be genuinely effective, it is preferable to pronounce or to sing them with an altruistic goal, with mind and heart turned towards the highest visualizations of cosmic love. The thirst for this absolute love, provoked by the singing of the Sacred Names, represents one of the most energetic means of adapting our own vibratory rate to that of the superior plains, inaccessible to the purely physical senses and powers of reasoning. This magical song can be freely practised by anyone, whether earthly, extraterrestrial or intra-terrestrial.

Just as there is no limit to genuine love, there are absolutely no bounds to the initiatory emotion of singing the Sacred Names; whether we are in the superior, inferior or intermediary universe, or whether we have the possibility to travel from one to another through our mechanical or mystical powers, each and every one of us can find in this song the greatest well-being and the greatest benefit.

CHAPTER 5

THE MUSIC OF THE AGE OF AQUARIUS

"Physicists have understood that reality is stranger than it seems, but this information has not yet reached biological sciences. Physicians fear physicists. They have never really thought of this marvellous and strange phenomenon: that for the most part, the atom is composed of space and that it consists of particles of frozen energy. The body is also frozen energy. This is very disconcerting for our physical senses. In a sense, this reminds us of the resistance of contemporaries of Pasteur, when he suggested the existence of the influence of invisible agents... Later, when the microscope was widely used and when the theory of germs had been proven, people accepted the fact that bacteria could be the source of illnesses, sterilization became a widespread practice in surgery and infections became much more controllable. Today, we have come to the point where we must prove the existence of new invisible influences and we should invent a technology which, like the microscope in the past, will allow us to prove the theory. During the next decade, we will be able to conduct very significant experiments which will validate this energetic medicine."

Dr. Richard Gerber
author of the book
Vibrational Medicine

"It is only when mastery and tranquility will have been acquired that the protectors of the race will make known to the world the music referred to as Buddhistic which will give us access, without danger, to an inner enlightenment whose grandeur will go beyond all that we presently know of what is most beautiful on Earth. This music will in some way resemble the mantram... The composer of this new musical era will invoke through music the entities of superior plains."

Cyril Scott
The Music

171

What is the Age of Aquarius?

The year 2,000 is at hand.

We are living at a time when a cosmic year is ending. Every 2,000 years (more precisely every 21 centuries), Earth changes eras, which means that it penetrates into a new celestial sign of the zodiac. And in fact, we are living in a period when a zodiacal year is dawning: the new planetary spring where the sign of Aquarius replaces the age of Pisces. Humanity, in the course of its cyclical evolution, has known, and will come to know once again, the age of Cancer, the age of Leo, the age of Taurus, the Aries era, the spirit of Scorpio, of Sagittarius, of Capricorn, of Virgo, the eras of Libra and of Gemini and in each cycle, the world is submitted to the influences peculiar to the sign of the zodiac under which it evolves. It is thus that civilizations collapse, cultures change and that Earth is renewed. The spirit of Taurus brought with it new impulses, that of Aries was characterized by ambition and the desire to dominate. Millenia flow by, unfurl and all is transformed. Christ, the Universal Guide, appeared at the beginning of the Pisces era and showed the path to inner contemplation: "First seek enlightenment and everything will be given to you in addition". Some have succeeded the transformation.

Today, the sun, in its endless trajectory, touches with its rays the powerful sign of Aquarius, which will last until the year 4,000. All values are shifting. This is an enormous transition: from now on, we will turn towards spiritual identity, towards Nature and towards the Being on Whom everything rests. It is the end of a world for those who cling to dying values. The spirit of Aquarius does not seek the Christic principle out of respect, fear or nostalgia. It accomplishes

173

the divine within itself and realizes the Universal Soul in itself to better serve it. Love is the only power, the spirit, the tool of mastery. The new Atlantis will resurface, purified of past errors. A new World Guide offers universal consciousness. It is the age of unity, of breaking down borders and ''walls''... breaking down destructive egoism. Warriors are pacific and man, through intuition, freely directs his destiny with only the power of his mental vision.

Science finally breaks free of sensory concepts and discovers the cosmos' subtle energy systems and the Great Unifying Theory. Contact is made with intelligent life from elsewhere. Rhythms change and those who adapt to the new Aquarian spiritual waves will successfully live through this upsetting transition in order to beget the new universal solar man / woman. The music of the soul, the ''Atlantis Angelis'' which dwells in each of us, represents the power which exists soley to help us in successfully completing this unavoidable and necessary transformation. Musical energies harmonized with the formidable Aquarian influence are specifically studied to ensure constant contemplation of what is inalterable within us. Without this magical, secret, invisible but real work, we cannot successfully cross the threshold of this turning-point where the acceleration and intensity of cosmic energies are such that those who will choose not to attune themselves to the harmonics of the new infinite current and who choose not to identify with the recent pulsation of the Universe (whose impact on the world is already unprecedented), will simply be transferred to other levels of evolution.

No one will succeed in quieting the rhythm and the voice of renewed universality; no one will halt the Rebirth of Pure Music: one cannot stop the cosmic river of human history.

Uniting with the new harmony

Music created with the goal of vivifying the soul is the spirit's nourishment because it is not competitive. Its aim is elevation, not exploitation. In this musical approach, composer and listener are accomplices with the same desire for verticality, the same impetus towards the universal centre, the source of all things. It does not inflame the senses, but represents an invitation to meditation and devotion.

Music created with the goal of competing strengthens the ego and, consequently, tends to tighten the emotional knots which block us and prevent good energies from circulating freely within us. It is an enervating music; it shows digital skill and displays a form of sensuality so heavy that it imprisons and prohibits the liberation of the spirit. On the contrary, music composed with the goal of elevation is a releasing vibration; through it, the entities of the superior plains are invoked. It represents a sincere effort, directed towards the realization of light, peace and harmony. It relaxes, disentangles, dissolves anguish and anxieties produced by the illusions of the physical plain. It is also a sensual music, but its sensuality is sublime and is directed towards the organs of superior senses. It provokes a subtle and incomparable pleasure because it puts us into contact with the powers "Beyond", which are existence, consciousness and supreme happiness. This inner music makes it possible to taste greater serenity of the heart and to develop better mastery of the four bodies: physical, emotional, mental and etherial. We can see in it the premises of Buddhistic music, which gives the entire being access to enlightenment, the latter going beyond and transcending the realm of the known.

To enjoy this exceptional musical material, it is recommended that one enter a state of pure abandon of the self. A great number of relaxation techniques provide access to such a state. The music of the Age of Aquarius, by prolonging thought and allowing immediate muscular hypotonicity (the first stage of genuine relaxation), constitutes an inducing element of choice for complete and profound relaxation.

For the consciousness to free itself, it is good to "disconnect" the mental. A preoccupied mind cannot experience a state of availability, the *sine qua non* of effective musical perception. It is good also to develop a docile attitude towards the grace which sums up the art of entering into contact with such music. In order not to interfere with, or even interrupt, intimate listening, all obstacles to self-abandon should be eliminated gradually. It is only after this necessary transformation that we will see our emotions coincide with those of the music. In going beyond the ego, we will be capable of uniting with the new harmony.

The intemporal centre

It is a matter of finding the secret role of music, its real function. It is said to soothe the savage beast; this is true: music holds this power. It can transform a barbarian into an evolved being. It can also transform an innocent person into a blood-thirsty savage. Not all sound energy is fit for listening and it is possible that only energy which "soothes our manner of living" deserves to be described as mystical music.

Music is deemed to bring harmony to the subtle bodies of men, levelling the "ways of the Lord", preparing and facilitating the advent of the instructors of this world. The music of the soul is a conscious vibration, a Buddhistic energy whose role is to enlighten the entire being. It corresponds to ridding the physical body, the spiritual heart and the whole spirit from all forms of parasite. It addresses itself directly to the soul and comes from the soul, thus transcending the physical, mental and intellectual plains. It provokes a controlled trance, which calmly sets in motion a process of removal from the fight for existence which goes on at the level of matter. It puts our individual and collective conflicts into perspective by linking us to superior spheres and worlds. It is in itself religion in the Latin sense of the word *religare* or to bind. It has the power to link us to the cosmos by building a bridge of light between our solitude and the multitude of celestial hierarchies, always ready to come to our assistance. It is the divine name and number as infinite energy and it represents the miracle of perfect healing. It undertakes to draw us nearer to ourselves and closer to the Inner God.

When music does not help us recover our true identity, when it removes us from our constitutional state, it does not fulfill its function and becomes a simple form of entertainment. The music of the Age of Aquarius is the music of the soul in the sense that it refines the thought process; and it is in this sense that it offers us time, which we urgently need, to recover the intemporal centre vibrating in each of us. Upon contact with it, we automatically review our priorities. The musical vibration effects a polarity change in our values. Instead of putting all our efforts into ''having'', in listening to it, we develop the ability to value ''being'' anew. The result is a reharmonization of the body, the heart and the goal of existence. Problems related to form (physical, mental, emotional and etherial bodies), then take on less importance and we take into consideration fundamental problems (the soul's eternal life), and this results in a net reduction in existential stress. This progression allows us to discover our true harmonic identity.

Freedom and responsibility

With the advent of the Age of Aquarius, which is also the age of understanding of the words ''freedom'' and ''responsibility'', embarking on a crusade against a particular type of music will be out of the question; rather, the time will have come to observe, inquire and become more familiar with the functioning of the mysterious world of music and sound energies and to become fully aware of the implications, for us, of listening and hearing a given type of music. It will also be a matter of giving ourselves the option of getting to know a little more about the invisible vibrations ''which affect us so much''. Lévi-Strauss writes:

> ''Music represents the supreme mystery of human knowledge. All other fields of knowledge are integrated into it. Music holds the key to their progress.''

This mystery can be unveiled, but the music ''itself'' must so wish, for it is a living being, which seeks respect and love. Therefore, it is essential to love and respect this being, which is all too often but a means of subsistence or a source of excitement, if not simply a stimulus to help sell the insignificant.

The Atlantean angels

Music does not come to us through exploitation, but rather through dedication. One cannot exploit a high priestess; on the contrary, one endeavours to serve her respectfully and lovingly. Consequently she notices us and vests us with her supra-natural powers. For anyone who has never seen an airplane, the laws of aerodynamics are magical. In the same manner, the musicians of the new era will be seen as magicians. They will be conscious of the laws of sound and will apply them. They will be conscious of the magical function of melodies on the body and spirit of man. They will use it in a positive and constructive manner, for the greater good of humanity. Thus, they will save the world. These musicians have already begun to rediscover this power. They use musical energies to create harmonious forms which are of a nature to elevate the soul and inspire beautiful and noble thoughts. Therefore, they are beneficial to all the living beings of the universe, for the vibration cannot be destroyed.

Once emitted, a sound goes on eternally and travels through the cosmos, influencing all the beings it encounters. By following this path, the musicians of the new era avoid the mistakes of the priests of ancient Atlantis, who had understood that **one can put certain powers into action and obtain tangible results through repetition of certain combinations of notes**. Esoterical tradition teaches us that these priests had put their science in the service of destructive forces. They misused their knowledge and the powers they were capable of putting into action. In this way, discordance was voluntarily used to beget disintegration, which resulted in the fall of the Atlantean continent. But the occult history of the world will not repeat itself. The magician-musicians of the new era will bring Atlantis back to life through the impact of their inventions and this new Atlantis will know an atmosphere of angelic light. The science of sounds will not be used with the aim of demolition, but rather it will be specifically calculated to accompany a state of cosmic consciousness or union with the Divine. From these musical creations will emanate the breath of divine harmony.

The true goal of the music of humans

Why do we listen to music? What are we really seeking? As we have seen, according to the tradition of Vedanta, the goal of life is to dedicate ourselves to our own evolution and to elevate ourselves to the plain of divine love. If we reason logically, music should help us in this regard. But in the history of humankind, the world has never known a period as violent as ours. One need only glance at a newspaper for proof. The sounds and musical energies produced by the modern world are often at the origin of such a state of things. But what injures can also heal. And by softening our mores, the new music of the soul **brings us world peace and purifies the aura of the planet**.

Currently, humanity's greatest need is to rediscover the true goal of music. To enter into contact with the soul and elevate consciousness to the level of transcendence until a perfect state is reached: such is the true goal of the music of humans, such is the role of the music of the new age.

A surge of good sense

Humanity is about to rediscover the cosmic role of sound. Malraux was right in saying: "The 21st Century will be spiritual or it will not be." The choice is proportionate to life. The positive vision shows us the direction that humanity will take, the only possible alternative being to follow the course of its evolution. It is possible to believe that in a surge of good sense, the human race will decide not to self-destruct. First will come freedom from noise and all debilitating sound vibrations. Then, we will rediscover the music of the soul, solely capable of reconnecting us with our profound intuitions, of offering us the opportunity to taste anew the nectar of the inner source. Through it, humankind will once again hear the music of heaven.

Today, meditative listening to music has already been rediscovered. It is a sign of the times. The first step has been taken. Although sometimes closer to birth than maturity, it announces the Age of Aquarius and conspires against reductionism and fanatical materialism. Its true sense as well as its impact on the intimate being is yet to be discovered, to be redefined, so that the ability to profoundly listen to life may be rediscovered.

Already, pioneers are clearing the way everywhere in the world. One of the most beautiful examples is undoubtedly the experience conducted by Georges Balan. This musicologist of Roumanian origin, a former professor of musical aesthetics at the Bucharest Academy, has studied these problems in detail. His views have led to the foundation of the Musicosophia movement, whose centre is The Institute for the Spiritual Analysis of Music and for Training in Conscious Musical Listening. Its activities are aimed at making it possible for the listener to discover his specific mission and to initiate him – whatever his training or knowledge of music may be – to the art of profound listening. Such experiments are worthy of note. Let us hope that this kind of school will be founded in all parts of the world. In an interview given to *Third Millenium* magazine (Troisième Millénaire) and devoted to the art of musical listening, Georges Balan declared:

> "I have always been astonished by the obvious disagreement between what the great masters wished – that their works elevate man and render him conscious of the eternity he bears within him – and the poor repercussions of these works in the consciousness of listeners, usually only attracted by music's sound structure and its sentimentality."

The magical and meditative work

We must go further in listening if we wish to penetrate the infinite realm of sounds. Immense efforts, through which the power of harmony succeeds in speaking to us in a sometimes disturbing manner, take on meaning in so far as they awaken in us the will to feel this energy as intensely as it is felt by those who transmit it to us.

In other words, sounds will reveal nothing to us as long as we have not yet discovered the ''listener's'' mission **whose creative contribution is at least as necessary as that of the composer and the performer**. When, under the action of sounds, purifying and liberating functions are carried out in our soul, the reason music exists, we truly achieve profound listening.

This is what the music of the new era provokes. These particular sound waves have the capacity to extend thought. They invite us to dive consciously into the depths of inner language. Music thus becomes the music of the soul, opening to it the doors to renewal of its own intimate life. When this faculty is not perceived, the spiritual value of this art collapses. All that remains is the echo, sometimes powerful, but always ephemeral or existential, of the sounds within us. Music is then relegated to one of the lesser degrees in the hierarchy of the arts. We draw from it only the current effect it produces in us, which is often but an evanescent sensual pleasure. This is still, alas, the true image of the general attitude towards melody, when it is taken only as entertainment. To perceive the music of the soul, this attitude must undergo a radical change. **The composer cannot accomplish the magical work alone; he needs the listener's complicity**. It is necessary that the latter concern himself with the redeeming and liberating message hidden in sounds. Without this vigilance on the part of the listener, the composer's task, which consists in revealing cosmic and supreme realities, is futile. It is only through this extreme vigilance that it is possible, on the one hand, for the composer to meet the listener and on the other hand, for the infinitesimal soul to meet the Supreme Soul...

Most of the time, the listener – who is also the meditator and the hearer – is passive because he is totally unaware of the essential role he plays in relation to the music, in relation to sounds and mantras. He imagines that the composer, or the creator of sounds, or the performer, can do all that is required on his own, without the listener having to lift his little finger!

It is to eliminate this terrible misunderstanding that an increasing number of composers are making themselves heard and attempting to restore to music its true function: **that of linking souls to other souls, and linking souls to God**.

The music of the soul, being in the prophetic sense of the word the music of new times, must automatically suppress the composer / listener misunderstanding. The education of both parties in this direction is absolutely necessary if we wish the message received by the composer from the highest regions of the spirit to be transmitted to the listener. The latter's responsibility is no less great than that of the former. In the same manner, the guide or guru-master, or warrior, or great kabire (as one wishes to call it) – when he is authentic – must find a disciple, himself authentically sincere in his approach, so that the message he transmits may be received, heard and retransmitted in turn.

Here is the eternal archetypal love relationship: guide / disciple, father / son, husband / wife, etc. The triangular relationship of composer / performer / listener is also a pure relationship, when the intent of the musical experience is of a superior nature. Without this particular intent, it remains at a base level; that is to say, it remains vaguely indifferent, sentimental, when it is not simply idolatrous. Musicologist Georges Balan, in his *Essay on Meditative Listening* (Essai sur l'écoute méditative) asks this important question:

> "Which listener is conscious of the inner work he must accomplish so that the creation (of the composer) and the recreation of the performer are truly fruitful?"

The work referred to here by Georges Balan is not the complacent delight we usually allow ourselves to enjoy. It is a work of conquest: **it is a matter of conquering the true joy of clairaudient musical listening**, a joy which has nothing in common with ordinary auditory sensations. The creative process ends when the message of joy triumphs in our inner life. During a feast, guests act directly so that the culinary creation reaches its goal: they eat. Thus, the listener who is invited to the table of music should not remain complacent, a mere spectator. He must seat himself at the table and must celebrate the great initiatory feast of the all-powerful Audible.

A path towards light

There is no other means for the spiritual essence of sounds to reverberate victoriously and lastingly within us. Beethoven has summarized this essence in the following terms:

> "An inner gushing forth of the fire of the spirit and an elevation of the soul above the misery where others crawl."

At this level, it is the soul of the listener which becomes his score and instrument. No musical science is required. However, what is absolutely necessary is the faculty of powerfully concentrating one's attention. The chanting of the *japa* and the living listening to the Sacred Names, in addition to purifying the mind and heart, can be extremely useful for whomever wishes to sharpen his concentration. Hearing the music of the soul is not a tawdry activity. It is the work of a warrior and it calls for a compassionate vigilance. It is enough for the listener to identify with a certain part of the music, for it to start acting within him like a living being with whom he can converse intimately. Then, the answers he receives will be revealing. Music will cease to be a mere distraction. Charged with the superior energy of supra-sensitive worlds, it will become the direct expression of such a lofty spiritual reality that the soul will not hesitate to attribute to it a divine meaning. However, Georges Balan adds:

> "if the listener has really entered into this intimate dialogue with the melody that sings within him, it is in a tender and affectionate manner that he experiences this majesty, sometimes terrible, of the spiritual world perceived as living beyond perceptible sounds."

In the near future, for us, music will be nothing else but a wise and friendly accomplice which will guide us towards the light and will help us exit from the darkness of the world's pain and illusion. Man will have no other choice but to take its message seriously, for he will have understood that it is the music he creates that builds the societies in which he lives. **By the sounds he emits and listens to, man is the master and the creator of his destiny.**

The new breath of consciousness

It is no longer possible to remain unaware of the incredible planetary transformation we are witnessing. The Earth's consciousness is about to experience a total revolution and the latter will serve to reharmonize humanity's priorities with the rest of the galaxy.

In his book *The Awakening Earth*, Peter Russel is unhesitant in declaring:

> "Something miraculous may be happening on this planet, on our tiny blue pearl. Humanity may well find itself on the threshold of an evolutionary step, a step that could happen with lightning-quick speed, a step such as happens only every billion years. And the change that is leading us towards this step is happening before our very eyes – or rather behind our eyes – in the depths of our own spirits."

With the same contagious optimism, Marilyn Ferguson writes in *The Aquarian Conspiracy*:

> "Even the Renaissance did not hold the promise of such radical renewal...We are linked by our travels and technology, more and more conscious of one another and open to one another. We are discovering that an increasing number of people can mutually enrich and reinforce themselves and that we are more attentive to our place in nature."

The new scientific circles are disrupting the old School of thought, still caught up in its specificity. Physicist Fritjof Capra says in *Time of Awakening*:

> "We need a new paradigm, a new vision of reality, a fundamental change in our thoughts, perceptions and values. The beginning of this change, of this passage from a mechanistic conception to a holistic conception of reality can already be seen in all fields and it would seem, will dominate the present decade."

It would seem that music has a crucial role to play in the advent of this new paradigm, of this new vision of the world. To create the Age of Aquarius, music must go beyond the level of naïve entertainment to reach the sphere of the spirit. It will be the breath of consciousness; it will become the song of souls by echoing their highest intuitions, it being so true that through it, the soul's life manifests itself in this world. New composers will once again hear the grandiose symphony vibrating in the galaxy and their creations will awaken the superior responsibility of the human form. Maestro Omraam Mikhaël Aïvanhov declared in a series of lectures on artistic creation:

"Music awakens in our soul the memory of the celestial fatherland, the nostalgia for a lost paradise. It is one of the most powerful vehicles, more powerful than painting or dance because it is immediate, instantaneous... We suddenly remember that we come from heaven and that it is to heaven that we must one day return. That there is music that, on the contrary, awakens in us the desire to remain on Earth is a fact; but such is not the genuine predestination of music."

The new composers will not only be virtuosos; they will be genuine mystics. Their mission will surpass the role of public entertainers and they will recover **the great initiatory work of the creators of sacred music**. In so far as their music will put human beings into contact with the devic, edenic and spiritual spheres, they will allow men to once again hear the great cosmic breath and to physically feel the supra-natural presence that each of us bears within us through eternity.

Uniting with the great Devas

Instead of simple virtuosos, whose predominating influence has always shown the signs of the decadence of music, we will encounter truly inspired artists. The latter will show no interest in embellishments devoid of any musical content and will draw closer to rich and inspired melodies which, while they may not excite the crowd's enthusiasm as virtuosity can, will have the specific power to emit strong and subtle vibrations which will penetrate and move the soul by opening hearts and awakening minds. In his *History of Music*, Naumann describes the musical degeneration which regularly strikes men. In the case of ancient Greece, the situation is obvious and worthy of note. Music had degenerated to such an extent that only frills were important. The substance of musical experience and the message to be expressed were of no interest to anyone any longer. Naumann explains:

"Artifice supplanted art and sensation supplanted depth of feeling."

We now know that the state of a distinct musical language triggers a similar state in human society. Had this point not yet been assimilated, we would need only to examine the consequences of musical degeneration on the ancient Greek society. After this fall, history records a weakness in the character of the Greeks, proportionate to the changes occurring at the time. Also noted were a decline in the sense of morality and the "inexplicable" failure of all military operations. Then followed the interference of other nations in the social balance and a loss of the taste for independence: this marked the end of their prosperity.

Contemporary man, evidently no longer able to trust the perverted religious, puppet-politicians and sorcerer's apprentice-scientists, will turn towards artists to encourage them to compose a music capable of uniting suffering humanity with the Devas who preside over the affairs of the universe. Man must not only guide them in their inspirations, he must also act directly on the various milieus of the media, which continuously broadcast sounds, words and music and regardless of who they may be, are the ferment of the future in so far as these waves literally sculpt the environment of tomorrow.

The great clairvoyant Cyril Scott points out in his cult book on *Music and its Secret Influence Through the Ages*:

"Tomorrow's music will have the mission of putting us in closer contact with the world of the Devas, thus making it possible for regular concert-goers to benefit from the protection of these great Beings, invoked with the help of the harmonization of appropriate sounds."

The scientifically adapted music which Scott refers to here, will have precisely the role played by the great *mantram* of Antiquity's initiatory ceremonies of the Vedic and Atlantean periods: that of invoking the Devas. Moreover, in the conscious listener, these mantric musical energies will stimulate the faculties through which it will be given to him to answer the incredible vibratory speed of these individuals from elsewhere, from other regions of the Universe not perceived by our imperfect senses. Man should put aside his arrogance towards nature and reharmonize himself with it; if not, he will be eliminated by apocalyptic events which he will inevitably be a powerless witness of, if he stubbornly continues the anarchic exploitation of the planet's non-renewable resources. These great upheavals, (climatic changes, the melting of the ice-cap, generalized earthquakes, global droughts, etc.) will only be the result of his criminal actions towards animals, the Earth, human beings, the four elements, the spirits of nature, elves, fairies, gnomes and heaven's angels.

The effect of a revelation

The message of the music of the new times does not solely address our senses or our mental powers, as is so often the case of the music proposed by the current system. By directly addressing our eternal being, the harmonies of the Age of Aquarius will open the doors of spiritual freedom. Through a unique type of synthesis, they will link the most basic substance of the living soul to the most glorious plains of the spiritual worlds. As Beethoven predicted, music will have the effect of a revelation on the soul. When man will discover, through the action of sound waves, that **he and the Global Being are of the same essence, the same nature, possessing, for all eternity, the same qualities,** he will no longer be limited to the bottom rungs of the ladder of his evolution and will rapidly reach the levels of superior initiations. Purified sound energy will carry him to his original fatherland, towards his true identity, and he will recover his constitutional position within creation. Thus, he will be liberated from fear, hatred, rebirth, old age, illness, from the transfer of physical death and from all contingencies associated with the world of matter.

The individual who genuinely enters into the symphony of the new age simultaneously sets aside all supplicating and grovelling attitudes. He rises above the human condition and sings, with intelligent faith, a song of praise based on the knowledge of the laws governing the universe rather than on a given belief. **He no longer believes: he is aware; he no longer hopes: he knows.** His doubts are reduced to nothing by the triple fire of knowledge, silent joy and inner vision.

The music of the soul – this irresistible intimate song which moves the mountains of boredom and despair – restores strength and courage; and the individual who strives to hear it, is directed by celestial powers towards earthly guides. These living masters teach through example; every sincere seeker can be sure of finding one on his path. The assistance of these guides is precious. The music of the soul can be perceived by means of inspired meditative song or some sacred music belonging to a category said to be ''classical''. Likewise, works judged folkloric or ''primitive'' are, in fact, great sound bridges leading directly to profound listening.

At this level, we rapidly see that the labels attributed to certain musical types have only a relative value. Truly, if it is of a meditative character or of superior inspiration, it can make the soul tremble and can provoke, through intuition, the awakening of the quiver of inner life. Psychological scars are more or less deep and each of us reacts differently. Prejudices – terrible preconceived ideas which block the energies of the heart – take root in the mind and some individuals must wait years, even lifetimes, to feel the undefinable something in their inner self which, most of the time, is perceived as an unforgettable movement of the depths of the conscience. Others are fully awakened to the Reality of these intimate unlimited spaces.

What can trigger the mystical experience of the music of the soul most rapidly is listening to and chanting the Sacred Names as they are transmitted to us through tradition – or, if we have rejected tradition, as frequently is the case – as they have been revealed to us through a master, a dream, a book, an inspiration or as simply brought by highly evolved entities from space or from plains of parallel existence.

The *"guru-shastra-sadhu"* formula

It is good to authenticate one's evolutionary path in the universe of spiritual sound energies. To this end, the Sanskrit formula "*guru / shastra / sadhu*" can be very useful. To be certain of not taking the wrong path (pitfalls are as numerous as they are subtle) it is advisable to verify the cogency of one's personal approach with an authentic guide (*guru*) or with authoritative writings (*shastra*), or by studying the life and the teachings of the sages of the past (sadhu). When these three references coincide, one can be certain of not wasting time, of not losing one's way on approximate roads. **Blind faith always represents a danger and fanaticism is the enemy of truth**. On the other hand, when the authenticity of such a method of awakening has been proven through this formula, direct experimentation should not be avoided.

The criteria for the success of any technique for awakening the consciousness, and even more so for the successful search for the music of the soul, requires that it be practised directly and diligently, in a spirit of detachment and inner vigilance, free of all responsibilities related to any school of thought, past, present or future.

The music of the Age of Crystal

The Age of Aquarius lays rightful claim to the purity incarnated by crystal. To achieve the purity characteristic of quartz, unconditional love, love without expectation, divine love, must manifest its presence.

If love grows and develops, the way is authentic. Purified love represents the only criterion for advancement. No other criterion exists, since only divine love is liberal, tolerant and inclusive of all things. It is sufficient unto itself; it expects nothing, asks for nothing. It thrives on its own autonomy. The music of the soul is the music of this love. Pure love reveals divinity in the human soul; it is unlimited and its outcome can only be made known through visions. In his renowned book entitled *The Lives of the Masters* (La Vie des Maîtres), B. T. Spalding discusses genuine love in the following terms:

> "Love constantly seeks an opening to flow into the human heart and spread its blessings. If man's perversion and discordant thoughts do not divert it, the eternal and immutable river of God's love flows endlessly, bringing to the great universal ocean of oblivion, all that appears to be in disharmony, all that is ugly, all that is likely to disturb the peace of men. Love is the perfect fruit of the spirit. It comes forward to tend to humanity's wounds, to bring nations closer together in harmony and to bring to the world peace and prosperity. It is the rhythm, the very pulse of the world, the heartbeat of the Universe."

Love is inseparable from the life of the soul; it is the incarnation of the divine fruit which corresponds to the celestial food of the living being. Through it, the world will soon see the splendour of the Age of Crystal established on Earth. The music of the new composers will annihilate the spirit of limitation, borders, pettiness, still reigning in humanity's heart. By means of this music at once new and millenary, nations will extend their hand to the forces of the Spirit. **America will discover that the dove is more powerful than the eagle**. It will answer to the appeal of these spiritual waves. People will evolve through the sympathetic nervous system, using the forces of intuition, and not the cerebro-spinal nervous system which directs reason and the intellect. Music purified of the fears and demands of the negative ego, will reestablish perfect equilibrium between the right and the left side of the brain. Consequently, human beings will be more sensitive to new spiritual sound combinations and this sensitivity will be the result of the advent of spiritualized musical approaches.

All highly inspired musics vibrate to the rhythm of the inner force. They hold the power to save humanity from the lack of harmony which characterizes it. The music of the soul is this work of art which creates an emotion bearing the sensations of eternity. In listening to it, the hearer plunges into the feeling of something infinite. He experiences changes in his state of consciousness. These waves, of a spiritual nature, provoke within him certain circumstances under which the genuine mystic feeling reaches its highest point. He is thus bathed in a limitless oceanic environment and he penetrates into a mystic transpersonal experience which brings forth in him the flowing river of youth necessary to the crystallization of the great limpid feelings of love which carry the soul to the threshold of its own ecstasy and its own immortality.

The Age of Unity

The human being who listens to the music of the new times perceives the unity of the cosmos and perceives himself within this unity. While conscious of being at One with the galaxy, he still does not lose his spiritual identity; become One with all that surrounds him, he still remains simultaneously different. This form of enlightenment is accompanied by an unqualified feeling of peace and universal unity, without demands and without needs.

Conscious of being the soul and not the body, the entity who listens profoundly perceives the illusory and ephemeral character of this world and abandons the worry of penury and death. By addressing the heart-being, without using the brain-being as an intermediary, the music of the soul provides the opportunity of finding "oneself" between the inner spaces of its bars and notes. Stockhausen senses this need when he writes:

> "Our music has become a music of discourse. It has been determined by muscles: those of the larynx for singing, those of the fingers for keyboard instruments, those of respiration for wind instruments. Everything is determined by the body. This is why we have never followed rhythms faster or slower than the natural movements of the body. Rhythms of walking, the pulse, the heart, all the mechanical rhythms which are those of the body, which send us back to the body and not to something free, which flies, which lets me rediscover between the bars of the music my own rhythm, which gives me time; something that changes, that is not static, that has the faculty of variation that I cannot find in the mechanical life of everday."

The new music of the Age of Aquarius represents this "something that flies": it is submersion in the absolute present, it is a halt and meditation on a sound. This "halt" makes it possible to expand consciousness. By expanding consciousness, it expands hearts. This expansion will gradually allow the manifestation of the supra-mental on Earth, the descent of universal light into hearts and the advent of Unity.

The musical bath of the Song of the Universal

To feel the forces of music linked to the power of the Sacred Names better, I suggest an exercise involving the use of "**The Song of the Universal**", (on the "ying" side of "**Atlantis Angelis**"). Of course, this exercise can be practised with any music belonging to the field of inspired meditative song. However, "**The Song of the Universal**" featured on "**Atlantis Angelis**" is especially appropriate. This can be explained by the choice of particular resonances as well as by the very nature of the mantric language used and the pure intent it holds. Practise it each day and you will experience a profound inner transformation in the most subtle regions of your being.

This exercise does not involve mental effort, nor does it involve the will and even less does it involve the intellect; it calls for imagination, which is man's prime faculty, as proven by Émile Coué, the father of autosuggestion and positive assertion. Imagination! Gisèle Robert, a Gestalt psychotherapist and a therapist who uses mental imagery, made the following statements in the November-December 1989 issue of *Resource Guide* Magazine:

> "Mental imagery calls on the capacity we all have to gain access to information hidden deep within us... Research has proven that a neurophysiological process is triggered in the organism not only when we experience a concrete situation, but also when we imagine it. As if the body were unable to distinguish fact from fiction, reacting to both in the same way. A difficult situation experienced during a nightmare, for instance, will make us perspire as much as a real event. Why should it not be the same for positive emotions? Thus, a person who will imagine himself or herself in a golden light will be strengthened by the light's healing powers."

30 minutes of liberation

At the beginning of the exercise, listen to "**The Song of the Universal**", comfortably seated, or lying down in a relaxing position (feet slightly apart, arms along the body, hands relaxed). Those who already practise the *astanga-yoga* or a form of *hatha-yoga*, can practise *padmasana*.

Breathe slowly, deeply, while relaxing each of your muscles, one after the other. At first, do nothing, do not think. This may seem simple enough, but it truly demands a certain state of grace. Imagine that your mind liberates itself from all thoughts that can congest it.

If you directly feel the benefits, you can softly repeat a short sentence of positive autosuggestion to unhypnotize the mental from negative illusions. For example: "I feel completely relaxed. From now on, everything will go well. I am a friend of the universe and the universe supports me". While repeating this short sentence, abandon your everyday worries, "let them fall". Offer your soul 30 minutes of liberation. Suspend the powers of your body and your mind. Give them freedom. Do not immediately begin working with the music. Let it penetrate you without really listening to it. It is there and like an intimate friend, it offers you its presence. You both feel good. All is peaceful.

At this point, the exercise requires a mental gesture which goes in search of the music. To feel it and listen is no longer sufficient: **it is necessary to go towards it**. You must seek it, relate to it, attract it and introduce it into your body through the doors of the centres of energy (*chakras*). This is the very basic and easy work of the alchemist, which everyone can accomplish effortlessly and in which the mental power unites with the musical power to build a magnetic sound bridge. Music can then use this bridge to reach into the depths of the living being.

With a good mental outlook, this technique – which has also been developed under a different form by Professor Thomas Zébério, without the use of the initiatory energy of the Sacred Names – plays an active role in the self-liberation of psycho-physiological currents and procures superior physical and intellectual performance. But the true mission of this method consists in helping man to reach a state of spiritual serenity such as he has never had the opportunity of experiencing previously.

A flame of compassion

After this first conscious contact, visualize at the level of the heart, a flame of compassion, small at first, but gently increasing in size. This fire of love eventually envelopes you completely. Feel the magnetic substance of the music traverse you. Now direct these musical energies towards the point of your body where you know a blockage exists. You can feel it. It could be a physical injury or a psychological hurt. Lay the music on your solar plexus and in your imagination, allow it to penetrate you. When you feel its action, visualize all the noxious body fluids which block the heart's entrance, and feel them adhering to the magnetic substance of the sound. It is possible that you may feel a type of pain due to the shift in negative energy; but it will disappear with the evacuation of these body fluids. This stage of the exercise is similar to a musical shower.

Be conscious that the thought and spiritual energies emitted by the composer unite with the modulations of the music that penetrates you. This thought helps you in your work, it supports and influences you. It is necessary to be selective in what we listen to **because the thoughts which permeate music truly penetrate us and act upon us**. When the composer's intention (and, if such is the case, the performer's) is directed towards the good, the beautiful and the true, the result is particularly beneficial. It is important that the sole motivation underlying the creation of a composition be the purification and the elevation of the world. The intentional energy which permeates music is virtually indelibly carved into our subconscious. Let us be selective in what we listen to!

To return to our exercise involving a meditative musical bath, literally seek the music and lay it on your solar plexus. Make it penetrate deeply; let it act on its own. The mantras composed of ''**The Song of the Universal**'' are powerful; let them softly do their healing work. These mantras heal from the inside your deepest psychological

194

wounds, they cure your sentimental injuries and smooth the subtle tissues of your heart, so long battered by the illusions of exterior energy.

In particular, the first mantra of "**The Song of the Universal**", the *Radha-madhava mantra*, is the sound personification of pure love without expectation. The power of this love is incommensurate. The life of those who experience it, even in an infinitesimal fraction, can never be the same again. The *radha-madhava mantra* is a sound vibration capable of producing a state of ecstasy. Chronic illnesses can be cured by the strength of this mantra. **It creates powerful spiritual waves, divine waves proceeding directly from the superior plain**.

When we bathe in inner music, in the pure waters of sound energies, all negative miasma which ruin our existence are genuinely drained outward. The inner mantra's wave penetrates into the listener's physical and astral bodies and removes sufferings at the root. Then, once this cleansing is accomplished, this inner wave fills the cells with pure *sattva* (superior virtue) and with *para-shakti* (spiritual energy). It is a jolting song and it has the faculty of awakening the pineal gland as well as the faculty of killing all astral parasites without exception.

What the conscious may think at that time is of no importance. If the musical formula is played long enough and at a sufficient level for the ear to hear its words, it penetrates into the subconscious. When the latter has registered its words, it memorizes the data in the supraconscious (unconscious), which gradually influences the conscious by "removing the dust on the mirror of the mental". The result is an extraordinary awareness: awareness of the Self, awareness of the Inner God, awareness of the soul's place in the cosmos. Therefore, the external action of the sound and the internal action of the subconscious react to the sound. These two actions are not added to one another, but are multiplied and it has been established that an exponential force is thus unleashed.

I have noticed that it is not really necessary to understand the meaning of the words heard. In every case, they have an effect. In fact, superior energy is often more active when the consciousness is not active, since then no mental barriers exist. When reason is quiet, intuition talks. Whether we intellectually understand why fire burns or not, it continues to burn. What is true of fire is also true of sound. The *Radha-Madhava mantra* is a vibration which allows the listener to come into contact with his own soul and to leave illusion behind. It represents the Angelus of spiritual worlds. It erases karma. A highly powerful wave, it acts upon the entire body and the entire mind, cleansing our inner ''resonator'' and re-establishing the equilibrium in our cells. These waves help us achieve harmony with the universe.

A sphere of light and love

After this musical shower, above the flame of compassion and love which now surrounds you like a cylinder of living light, visualize a gigantic sphere of energy, of universal musical peace. The music of this sphere and the music you are listening to, merge. From this harmonic fusion, it is possible for you to draw as much light and love as you desire. This reserve of sound energy is infinite and night and day, is at everyone's disposal. Freely, without expecting anything in return, it continuously offers its support to those who seek it. Make this all-powerful energy slowly descend into the depths of your being – and feel how it permeates you, how it provides delicious well-being. Lead the music-light of peace and love towards the heart. Introduce it directly inside your heart and maintain it there for a few minutes. Then, open your heart. At this moment, the music spreads throughout your body, producing complete relaxation and providing a feeling of overall well-being as it is rarely experienced.

An aura of gold and harmony

All your centres of energy are permeated with this light of love and they delicately open, like flowers. At this moment, visualize a harmonic aural vapour, marvellously clear and golden, enveloping all your being. Bathe in this golden harmony. Feel each of your cells

196

absorbing it and feel that, under its impact, they quiver with joy. Then, lead it into all your limbs. Begin with your toes, your feet, your ankles, your legs and gradually go to the top of your head. This draining action is so powerful that it sometimes happens that the expulsion of negative psychological substances and the loosening of deep-rooted knots of anxiety trigger tears, emotional upheavals, uncontrollable laughter, etc.

Each person's reaction is unique and is always very personal. It happens also – because of the extreme tightening of the astral body's energetic centres – that no external reaction is manifested. Regardless of what happens at this stage of the exercise, one should not maintain within the desires of expression as they present themselves. One should not lose sight of **the goal of the exercise, namely to eliminate the noxious miasma of worries, fear, frustration and anger which prohibit the spiritual development of the soul, by blocking the** *chakras* . These pathogenic matters, composed of gross etherial elements, clog the being's energetic system and prevent the free circulation of superior energies. In this state, mystical experiences and the being's penetration of the invisible, reveal themselves to be impossible. This chronic state of sickness regularly gives birth to a sad society, grossly perverted, where the crime rate, violence and suicides reach levels beyond imagination. This is in no way surprising. With no perception whatsoever of worlds which transcend matter, no vision of the splendid beings who inhabit them, no ability to listen profoundly to the music of the stars, no contact with the elements of high vibratory speed in creation, and experiencing only a minute fraction of human feelings, why would modern man not deny the affairs of the spirit? He has not the remotest notion of them, since he finds himself separated from them by the wall of his chronic anxiety and indifference.

The negative substances of frustration and latent pessimism block access to the superior plains and prevent the perception of the inviolable laws of justice which govern the universe. This justice includes the marvellous yet terrible law of cause and effect. Having neither awareness nor knowledge of it (education at this level is more than laughable), modern man purely and simply denies it, to his greatest misfortune, without knowing that karmic law (each action leads to a corresponding reaction) prepares his future destiny with the greatest precision it is possible to imagine.

The serenity of Mother-Earth

It is useful to bear in mind that musical self-cleansing is minimal if not accompanied by slow and profound breathing. To end the musical bath, use your mental vision to direct your inner light towards all living beings: plants, flowers, trees, animals, stones, crystals, towards our brethren, the spirits of nature, towards water, fire, air and sun and towards the entire planet. The Earth – a living being – will quiver with happiness and will welcome the luminous energy you send it. It will allow it to spread throughout its entire body, will envelope it with serenity and will lovingly project it towards you. Accept it, charged with Mother-Earth's serenity and from then on, realize that we, living beings, citizens of the Universe, are not only a physical body but that we live "in" the body or, more precisely, "with" it. Realize that we are not the mental, but that the mental is there for our use (although most of the time the mental uses us...). Through superior intuition (*genuine buddhi*), feel how we are the *Atma*, the eternal soul.

This intuition produces such beautiful music that it is possible to physically and spiritually feel an immense ray of happiness and joy invading our entire organism. From this point on, you forgive yourself and you forgive those who have hurt you through their actions and words. From this total forgiveness, liberty is born. From this unlimited joy springs forth a flow of limpid, luminous youth, which invades each of your cells. From this point on, the state of perfect happiness can manifest itself, the happiness of the ethereal, emotional and physical bodies. It is this global, holistic happiness which is at the origin of the constitutional state of divine independence. This conscious state of happiness is indestructible and represents the highest secret of the music of the soul.

CONCLUSION

SOLARIS UNIVERSALIS:
THE ADVENT OF THE UNIVERSAL SOLAR BEING

In the final analysis, only the means to reach plenitude and the way in which to liberate the soul by accelerating its growth are personal processes. Truth is universal and belongs to no one. The soul itself only seeks to establish its centre of permanent gravity. To do so, it can follow a multitude of different paths; all these roads travel through exactly the same levels of consciousness, the same transformations, whether they are arbitrarily called yoga, religion, alchemy, churches or movements.

The path of the music of the soul is not the only path, but it corresponds to the era we are now living in and has the characteristics of simplicity and practicality. It is spontaneous, free and joyful.

When the consciousness is fragmented, the organism is in conflict with itself. This state of anguish is born of duality, is the principal cause of all illnesses. The human body and mind are directed by a network of intelligence which has its roots in quantum reality, holistic and unified. This intelligence, this consciousness is the cause of man's well-being and salvation. The music of the soul is an energy of unification and integration. It begets new and different perceptions and sensations, and is for each of us at the origin of another life experience. It is through this other way of living, perceiving and feeling that the music of the soul will gradually introduce the world of the 21st century.

We are living in a time crucial for humanity's evolution. Everyone is aware of this fact. Contemporary man is facing a choice: he can re-establish his relationship with nature and rediscover the genuine values of existence, or...he can disappear.

In the famous Aztec calendar, in the middle of the Stone of the Sun, the figure of Tomatiuh, is the "Sun" of the fifth race, our race. This race is surrounded with four "Suns" which have preceded us and which have been destroyed by various cataclysms. These disasters were caused by the absence of unity, the lack of contact with essential life. Around this central figure representing our civilization, we clearly see, carved in the stone, the word "shaking". All the scholars of the soul have reached the conclusion that our world will end in the midst of nuclear fire and earthquakes.

If man remains entrapped in the illusion of separation and if he does not discover his unity with life, with the living universe, with Mother-Earth and with the cosmic intelligence, if he obstinately rejects the sacred bond that links him with the Spiritual Source and denies his divine power, he will be forced, inevitably, to confront the earthquakes of the planet. Man's lack of love makes the Earth tremble with cold. His acts of cruelty will make it tremble with wrath.

However, I have another vision of the word "shaking" and it reveals a totally contradictory aspect. The vibrations foretold by the synthesis of science, philosophy and art which is the Stone of the Sun, are always interpreted by specialists in light of the negative eventuality of a great and final cataclysm. In my opinion, this is a mistake. Even in the worst of the planetary storm that governments (ignoring the laws that govern nature) will not avoid imposing upon themselves, it is extremely important to preserve, at all costs, a positive vision of the equilibrium and harmony of the divine spheres. The inner sanctum can in no way be troubled by generalized seisms and the complete collapse of the monetary system.

When such events occur, it is only to make us reflect on the situation; these changes coincide with the desire of verticality, of the elevation and purification that the living being called "Earth" periodically feels. Whatever it may be, we can be sure that the word shaking also has a positive meaning. Instead of seeing in this prophesy seismic waves devastating a world doomed to die, why not imagine the powerful sound jolts provoked by the massive broadcast of the songs of love and light which are peculiar to the music of the soul?

Instead of visualizing earthquakes caused by the destructive vibrations of apocalyptic nuclear explosions, I prefer to project into the world a vision according to which **the entire Earth already vibrates under the unprecedented effect of the high frequencies of rediscovered divine music.** These powerful sound waves overwhelm the soul of things and beings: hearts open, intelligences awaken and people decide to do good, working towards the happiness of all living entities. Under the luminous influence of these cosmic love quakes, the entire Earth at last regains access to the opportunity to follow the path of compassion and to gradually achieve perfect enlightenment.

This is not a dream. In reality, a profound current has begun to animate the world. Without a particular ideology, without a particular party, human beings conspire for their common happiness in a spirit of tolerance. This happiness cannot be fully manifested without reactivating the essence of our superior energy, that is to say, without recontacting the Christic, Buddhistic, Krishnic presence which goes beyond all concepts, which is within us and which is us, regardless of the name we choose to give it. But this readjustment exposes us to the resistance of the regressive peoples of the dying era, who still grapple with industrial rapacity, violent pollution and the fanaticism of a given Church or School, refusing to acknowledge the evidence of the sons and daughters of the new era. However, the entity who keeps his senses and his spirit in constant contact with the Source has nothing to fear from this great confrontation.

The very sign of Aquarius is composed of two waves of form symbolizing the vibration of a new sound which reverberates across the entire sidereal space. This new sonority corresponds to the celestial harmony of the music of the soul and from now on, the solar man, freed from the yoke of egoïsm and fear, will associate himself with it.

It is a sign of the times. Musical energies inspired by the great beings of superior spheres proclaim the superiority of the heart: the cosmic spring of the Age of Aquarius has at last dawned! We have growing awareness of the infinite powers awakening within us and that our sole and eternal duty, our unique work, is to use them to further worldwide evolution. To awaken these powers and to put them in the service of the elevation of the soul: such is the genuine goal of human music which, when it comes from the unfathomable depths of the heart, becomes the only substance in the universe capable of satisfying our thirst for absolute love.

To reject nothing, but to engage all in the immortal entertainment of inner transformation, such is the veritable renunciation, the true surrender. The rest is but chatter and wasted energy. The rest is of no practical use. Not to merely foster contemplative existence, but to celebrate the love of daily life by putting the least vibration in the service of the authentic being, such is the sacred process through which the world must pass, whether willingly or not, if it really wishes to survive the far-reaching environmental crisis now confronting it on all fronts. Of this happy mission, of this joyous pledging will be born humanity's new electromagnetic body, whose face will reflect the plenitude of great accomplishments in the serenity of the accomplished work. This face, glowing with beauty, benevolence and strength, will be the face of the universal solar being.

Om Tat Sat.

GLOSSARY
of Sanskrit words

Atma: Minute energy particle, integral part and fragment of the Divine. The atma is the being in itself. It is different from the physical body, whose heart it inhabits, and constitutes the origin of consciousness. It has its own individuality similar to that of God and its form is of eternity, knowledge and felicity. It is distinct from God; it has the qualities or attributes of God, in minute quantity. It constitutes the marginal energy of the Divine, it can be influenced either by material energy or by spiritual energy. In Sanskrit, atma is the living being. It is also designated by the names *jivatma* (distinct soul) or *anuatma* (infinitesimal soul), depending on the aspect one wishes to emphasize.

Ashrama: Dwelling where the research of spiritual realization is practised.

Acarya: Literally: he who teaches through example. Authentically qualified spiritual Master. He must belong to a spiritual persuasion proceeding from a divine manifestation and must also transmit its original message without betraying it. He shows all beings the path to inner enlightenment and his life is the very example of his teachings. In a less specific sense, this word is used for certain individuals who have held the role of teacher and have had disciples under their guardianship.

Astanga-yoga: From asta: eight, and anga: part. Yoga method set by Patanjali and comprising eight stages: *yama, niyama, asana, pranayama, pratyahara, dharana, dhyana and samadhi*. It makes it possible to achieve the realization of the supreme Soul (*Paramatma*).

Buddhi: Intelligence. Conscience, mental attitude, one of the eight organs of the perfection of knowledge (*jnana*) and one of the five senses. Awakening of the knowledge of consciousness. Superior intuition.

Bhagavad-Gita: Bhagavan: Supreme Being or Blessed; gita: song. It is the "Song of the Supreme Blessed". Dialogue, put into writing by the Vyasadeva manifestation (*avatara*), between Krishna and Arjuna. The topic is the knowledge of Absolute Truth, of the original, natural and eternal condition of all distinct beings, of cosmic nature, of time and action. It forms the essence of all Vedic Scriptures and the preliminary study of the Srimad-Bhagavatam.

Bhakti yoga: Or buddhi yoga. The way of the bhakti's development, love of God, in its pure state, without the slightest hint of interested action (*karma*) or intellectual or philosophical (*jnana*) speculation. Final stage of yoga, as taught by the Bhagavad-Gita; it is practised through renunciation of the self to the Divine, through devotional activities, under the direction of an *acarya*.

Brahma-Samhita: Very ancient text in which Brahma, the one who receives from God the power to create everything in the universe, describes the form, the attributes and the "realm" of Absolute Truth, after the Supreme Being was revealed to him.

Brahma: First being created in the universe, author of the Brahma-Samhita.

Brahman : Or brahmajyoti, radiance emanating from Bhagavan's absolute Body and representing the impersonal aspect of Truth, or the first degree of realization of the Absolute.

Bija: Symbol-letter holding a specific power or representating the creative or evocative sound vibration of the energy-divinity it confines.

Bhakti: Love, devotion for the Divine; pledging of the being's purified senses to the service of Supreme senses.

Bhajan: Or Bhajana. Reunion of spiritualists singing together hymns and devotional songs in the divinity's honour.

Caitya-guru: Form under which the Truth guides from the interior. The spiritual master hidden in everyone's heart.

Caitanya: Caitanya Mahaprabhu: Avatar who came to India 500 years ago to teach the way to realization in light of the present age. He played the role of a bhakti-yogi in order to show how to reanimate the love for Him, love which he liberally distributed to all, inundating the East.

Chakra: Wheel, disk. In Kundalini-yoga (ascent of the spiritual energy), centre of consciousness or wheel of whirling energy (vortex-ring).

Deva : Being endowed with the power of governing a sector of the universal creation and attending to the needs of all beings.

Devanagaki: ''Language of the gods''. Text which has the advantage of being able to represent all sounds. Each syllable has a mystical value.

Guna: Sattva-guna (virtue), rajo-guna (passion) and tamo-guna (inertia). Various influences which illusionary energy exercises on beings and things. They determine the manner of being, of thinking and of acting of the soul they condition. It is through their interaction that creation, and the maintenance and destruction of the universe are accomplished. The word also means chain or string.

Guru: The one whose opinion is considered. Spiritual Leader (by extension). This title is equally given to the planet Jupiter, considered as the guru of divinities.

Haridasa: Haridasa Thakura. Grand Bhakti-yogi, disciple of Caitanya Mahaprabhu, who conferred upon him the title of "*namacarya*". Master of the song of the Sacred Names because of his strict vow to sing daily 300,000 times the Names of Absolute Truth.

Jiva: Or jiva-tattva. Category of the discinct beings (*atma*), integrating fragments and parts of the "Aum-God".

Jiva-Goswami: One of the six great sages of Vrndavana (a village in India where Krishna revealed his spiritual Entertainments 5,000 years ago).

Japa: Reciting, ecstatic technique consisting of the repetition of the Sacred Names or of a mantra; the japa is used to obtain concentration in meditative exercises. It can be recited aloud, sung, whispered or recited silently. It is destined to facilitate communion with the Divinity. Christian liturgy calls it "litany". In this exercise, the japa-yogi uses a rosary.

Krishna: "The One who attracts all beings towards Him", "The Infinitely Fascinating". Divinity considered as the Avatar of all divinities of the Hindu pantheon. He is most often represented as a young man of bluish-black complexion, magnificently adorned. He is The One who fully owns the six excellences: beauty, wealth, fame, power, wisdom and self-denial.

Kali-yuga: Age (*yuga*) of quarrels and hypocrisy, the last of a cycle of four (*maha-yuga*); it lasts 432,000 years. The one in which we now live began 5,000 years ago. It is essentially characterized by the progressive disappearance of spiritual principles in favour of the concern for material comfort.

Kirtana: Kirtanam. Collective song of spiritual sound vibrations, usually accompanied by various instruments.

Maya: That which does not exist. Illusory energy. Under its influence, the soul believes itself to be the Master of Creation, the Owner and Supreme Beneficiary. Identifying itself with material energy, that is to say with the body (the senses), the mental and material intelligence, the soul throws itself into the quest for inferior pleasures and chains itself to an even greater extent to the cycle of deaths and rebirths. Illusionary power of God, created in the world of appearances and concealing the "divine game".

Mantra: Sound vibration which liberates the human being by healing his mental blockages and his tendency towards the material.

Maha-mantra: 32-syllable mantra advocated by Caitanya for the age of Kali. This mantra not only holds the power to liberate the conditioned being from his material tendencies, it also awakens within him the divine love and ecstasy of inner life.

Mana or manas: Mental or subtle plain of thought. "Inner sense that centralizes and coordinates the facts belonging to sensitivity and creates the will to search for and to represent facts." (Louis Frédéric, Dictionary of Indian Civilization, Robert Laffont, 1987).

Naradi-muni: Great sage, son of Brahma, who travels everywhere, across material and spiritual plains, where he spreads the glories of the Supreme Soul by singing and playing his vina (string instrument).

Omkara: Or *pranava* or *Om*. Spiritual sound vibration representing the Absolute.

Para-prakrti: Prakrti: nature (literally, what is directed). There are two sorts of prakrtis: *apara-prakrti*, material nature, and *para-prakrti*, spiritual nature, that is to say the living being. These two natures are governed by the Supreme Nature of the Divine.

Paramatma: Supreme Soul. Emanation of the Absolute Being who lives in the heart of each living entity, in each atom of creation and even between atoms. This emanation constitutes the localized and omnipresent aspect of the Truth and represents the intermediary degree of realization.

Purana: "Ancient" Sanskrit texts, 18 in number, dealing with the world's creation and attributed by tradition to Vyasadeva. The principal Puranas most referred to are the Brahma-purana, the

Padma-purana, the Vishnu-purana, the Shiva-purana and the Bhagavat-purana.

Parampara: Spiritual filiation. It is said of a guide, a text, a teaching, a knowledge that they are paramparas when they concur with the sacred texts and the masters of authentic filiation, originating from the Source of knowledge.

Prema: Prem, preman – Pure Love. Love for all beings and especially the God-Source.

Rasa: Literally, soft sentiment. Word designating the intimate relationship uniting the soul with God. There are five main *rasas*: loving sentiment; parental affection; friendship; fraternity; the attitude of service; neutrality. The soul participates in the same nature as God and is One with Him in quality; it is at the absolute level, between the soul and the supreme spiritual Whole (the Sovereign Being) that the exchanges of rasas find their origin and also their total unfolding.

Raga: "Attraction" or "colour". "In painting, the *ragas* describe an emotional moment provoked either by external agents (morning, evening, night, rain, storms, wind, etc.) or inner sentiments (sadness, love, longing, etc.). They combine with colours and lines to provoke in the one who looks at the image, the awakening of a certain number of emotions. In music, it is the combination of modes and rhythms which must awaken in the listener diverse sensations and emotions." (Louis Frédéric, *Dictionary of Indian Civilization*, (Dictionnaire de la Civilisation indienne), Robert Laffont, 1987).

Ravana: Demonic being. He wanted to build a staircase to reach the edenic planets but while avoiding the task of qualifying himself for such a voyage. The avatar Ramacandra definitely ended Ravana's materialistic plans after the latter offended him by kidnapping his spouse, Sita.

Rama: "Inexhaustible Source of felicity". At the same time, it designates the avatara Ramacandra, an example of the perfect sovereign, and the manifestation of Balarama.

Sruti: The whole of revealed Scriptures directly from spiritual plains. A revealed Scripture is, in general, a Vedic Scripture or any other scripture of authority in the field of spiritual science (*smrti*), that is to say one which explains the nature of Truth or of the soul and the eternal relationship uniting them.

Sukadeva Goswami: First orator of the Srimad-Bhagavatam (Bhagavat-Purana).

Sadhana: Disciple who must follow a devotee during his meditation.

Sanatana-dharma: Natural and eternal function of the soul, which is to create a link with the Truth.

Veda: ''Knowledge'', ''Which has been seen by sages'', ''Revelation''. Vedic Scriptures: they comprise four Vedas (the Rk, the Yajus, the Sama and the Atharva), as well as the 108 Upanishads, which constitute their philosophical part and their complement: the 18 Puranas, the Vedanta-sutra (or Brahma-sutra, great philosophical treatise constituted of aphorisms on the nature of Absolute Truth and composed in the fashion of a conclusion to the Vedas) and the Srimad-Bhagavatam. In it, 5,000 years ago, the avatara Vyasadeva compiled the spiritual knowledge until then transmitted orally.

Yuga: Each of the four ages of a maha-yuga. A maha-yuga represents each of the one thousand cycles of the four ages (*satya, treta, dvapara and kali*), each lasting 4,320,000 years, covering the duration of one day of Brahma.

Note: For more details on the definition of Sanskrit words, the reader should refer to the works published by Bhaktivedanta Editions, 1976, 1977, 1978, Lucay-le-Mâle, 36 600 Valençay), as well as to the *Dictionary of Indian Civilization* (Dictionnaire de la Civilisation indienne) by Louis Frédéric, Robert Laffont, 1987.

BIBLIOGRAPHY

Aïvanov, Mikhaël, *Artistic Creation and Spiritual Creation* (Création artistique et Création spirituelle), Prosveta Publishers, 1985.

Author unknown, *The Accounts of a Russian Pilgrim*, (Récits d'un Pèlerin russe), de la Baconnière Ed., du Seuil Publishers, 1974.

Bence, Dr. L. and Méreaux, M., *Practical Guide to Musicotherapy* (Guide pratique de musicothérapie), Dangles Publishers, 1987.

Benenzon, Ronaldo, *Manual of Musicotherapy* (Manuel de musicothérapie), Privat Publishers, 1981.

Bhaktivedanta, Swami, *Bhagavad-Gita*, Bhaktivedanta Publishers, Paris, 1977.

Bible, *Psalms*.

Blofeld, John, *Mantras or the Power of Sacred Words* (Les Mantras ou la puissance des mots sacrés), Dervy-Livres, 1985.

Capra, Fritjof, *Time of Awakening* (Le temps du changement), du Rocher Publishers, 1983.

Campbell, Dom, *The Quest – Music as Healing, Introduction to the Musical Brain*, Theosophical Society in America, Spring 1989.

Cannavo, Richard and Hidalgo, Fred, *Words and Musics* (Paroles et musiques), de l'Arducaria Publishers, No. 15, February 1989.

Carton, Dr. Paul, *Laws of Healthy Life* (Les lois de la vie saine), Copyright by P. Carton, 1922.

Caya, Hélène, *From Sound Springs Light* (Du son jaillit la lumière), Denis J. Paradis Inc. Publishers, Montreal, 1987.

Coué, Emile, *Complete Works* (Oeuvres complètes), Astra Publishers, 1976.

De Candé, Roland, *The Invitation to Music* (L'Invitation à la musique), Du Seuil Publishers, Paris, 1980.

Diamond, John, *Your Body Does Not Lie*, Warner Books Inc., 1980.

Drolet, Chantal, and Sicotte, Anne-Marie, *"Nutrition that Kills"* ("L'alimentation qui tue") in Resource Guide, Vol. 4, No. 6, July-August 1989.

During, Jean, *Music and Ecstasy*, (Musique et extase), Albin Michel Publishers, Paris, 1988.

Ferguson, Marilyn, *The Aquarian Conspiracy*, (Les Enfants du Verseau. Pour un nouveau paradigme), Calmann-Lévy Publishers, 1981.

Govinda, Lama Anagarika, *Creative Meditation and Multidimentional Consciousness* (Méditation créatrice et conscience multidimentionnelle), Albin Michel Publishers, 1979.

Kuhne, Louis, *The New Science of Healing*, (La Nouvelle Science de guérir), Cevic Publishers, 1978.

Kushi, Aveline and Michio, *Macrobiotic Pregnancy and Care to the Newborn*, (Grossesse macrabiotique et soins au nouveau-né), Guy Trédaniel Publishers, 1986.

Lingerman, Hal A., *The Healing Energies of Music*, The Theosophical Publishing House, A Quest Book, 1983.

Little Philocaly of the Prayer of the Heart, (Petite Philocalie de la prière du coeur), du Seuil Publishers, 1979.

Maveric, Jean, *The Hermetic Medicine of plants*, (La médecine hermétique des plantes).

Mersenne, Father, *Universal Harmony*, (Harmonie universelle), published in 1535.

Osmont, Anne, *The Rhythm Creator of Forces and Forms*, (Le Rythme créateur de forces et de formes), des Champs-Elysées Publishers, 1942.

Podolsky, Edward, *The Doctor Prescribes Music*, Frederick A. Stockes, Co., New York, 1939.

Rudhyar, Dane, *The Magic of the Tone and the Art of Music*, (La magie du ton et l'art de la musique), Arista Publishers, 1985.

Russel, Peter, *The Global Brain*, J.P. Tarcher Inc., Los Angeles, 1983.

Schmidt, K.O., *Chance Does Not Exist*, (Le Hazard n'existe pas), Astra Publishers, 1956.

Scott, Cyril, *Music, its secret influence through the ages*, (La Musique, son influence secrète à travers les âges), de la Baconnière Publishers, 1984.

Spalding, Bairt T., *The Lives of the Masters*, (La Vie des Maîtres), Robert Laffont Publishers, 1972.

Stevens, S.S. and Varnshofsky, Fred., *Sound and Listening*, (Le son et l'audition), Time.

Tegtmeier, Ralph, *Guide to New Musics*, (Guide des musiques nouvelles), Le Souffle d'Or Publishers, 1988.

Tomatis, A. Alfred, *The Uterine Night*, (La Nuit utérine), Stock Publishers, 1981,1987.

Zébério, Pr. J. Thomas, *Sounds and Human Energy*, (Les Sons et l'énergie humaine), Courrier du livre, 1979.

Note: The titles of books written in French have been translated into English, even in cases where English translations may not be available as yet. Consequently, once translated, these publications may be distributed under another title. Moreover, in preparing this publication, the author has, for the most part, worked with French translations of reference books originally written in English. In such cases, both titles have been provided. In the case of reference sources available only in English, only the original title is provided.

Bibliographical References

Alper, Dr. Frank, *Exploring Atlantis 1-2-3*, Arizona Metaphysical Society, Phoenix, 1981.

Altghuler, I., *"The Past, Present and Future of Music Therapy"*, in Podolsky, E., *Music Therapy*, New York Philos Lib., 1953.

Aucher, Marie-Louise, *Sonorous Man*, (L'Homme sonore), Epi Publishers, Paris, 1983.

Bence, Léonce, and Méreaux, Max, *Music for Healing*, (La musique pour guérir), Van de Velve Publishers, 1988.

Bertholet, Dr. Ed., *Reincarnation*, (La Réincarnation), Pierre Guenillard Publishers, 1978.

Besant, Annie, *The Power of Thought*, (Le pouvoir de la pensée), Adyar Publishers, Paris, 1988.

Bhaktivedanta, Swami, *Chant and Be Happy*, Bhaktivedanta Book Trust, Los Angeles, 1982.

Bhaktivedanta, Swami Prabhupada, *Sri Namamrra*, B.B.T. Publishers, 1982.

Bô-Yin-Râ, *The Practice of the Mantras*, (La pratique des mantras), de Médicis Library, Paris, 1982.

Butor, M., *Words in Music*, <Les mots dans la musique (Musique en jeu)>» du Seuil Publishers, 1971.

Carton, Dr. Paul, *Treatise of Medicine, Nutrition and Natural Hygiene*, (Traité de Médecine, d'alimentation et d'hygiène naturiste), P. Carton, 1920.

Chopra, Deepak, *Quantum Healing*, Bantam Books, 1989.

Cotte, Roger J.V., *Music and Symbolism*, (Musique et symbolisme), Dangles Publishers, Saint-Jean de Braye, 1988.

Curry, A. E., *Drugs in Jazz and Rock Music*, Clin. Toxicol. United States, 1968.

Foglio, Hélène, *Sound Dynamics. Approach of the Sound Universe. Yoga, Sound and Prayer* (La dynamique du son. Approche de l'univers sonore. Yoga, son et prière), Courrier du livre, Paris, 1985.

Frédéric, Louis, *Dictionary of Indian Civilization* (Dictionnaire de la civilisation indienne), Robert Laffont Publishers, 1987.

Garfield, Laeh Maggie, *Sound Medicine*, Celestial Arts, Berkeley, Cal., 1987.

Gregorat, Claudio, *Music's Spiritual Experience* (L'expérience spirituelle de la musique), Centre Triades Publishers, Paris, 1980.

Guillot, J. and M.A. Jost, J., and Lecourt, E., *Musicotherapy and New Methods of Associating Techniques* (La Musicothérapie et les méthodes nouvelles d'association des techniques), EST Publishers, Paris, 1977.

Hamel, Peter Michael, *Through Music to the Self*, Element Books Ltd., 1978.

Hanish, Dr., *A Course in Harmony* (Cours d'harmonie), Aryana Publishers, Paris, 1967.

Heline, Corinne, *The Cosmic Harp*, New Age Bible and Philosophy Center, Santa Monica, 1986.

Huneau, Sophie, *Healing Musics*, (Les musiques qui guérissent), Retz Publishers, 1985.

Howard, W., *The Music and the Child* (La musique et l'enfant), P.U.F., Paris, 1963.

Kuhne, Louis, *The New Science of Healing* (La Nouvelle Science de guérir), Cevic Publishers, 1978.

Khan, Sufi Inayat, *Music*, Sh. Muhammad Ashraf, Lahore, 1971.

Lachat, Jean, *Musicotherapy* (Musicothérapie), Guérin Publishers, Montreal, 1981.

Maltz, Maswell, *Psycho-Cybernetics*, Wilshire Books Company, 1968.

McCellan, Randolf, *The Healing Forces of Music*, Amity House, New York, 1988.

Menuhin, Yehudi, and Curtis, W. Davis, *The Music of Man*, Methuen, 1979.

Mitdhell, John, *The Dimensions of Paradise*, Harper Row Publishers, San Francisco, 1988.

Monte Young (La), *Selected Writings: the Chant of Pram Nath: the sound is God* (Le Chant de Pram Nath: le son est Dieu), Esselier Publishers, Paris, 1971.

Ortmann, O., *Non Auditory Effect of Music*, in Schoen, p. 244-245.

Quertant, G., *Music and Medicine* (Musique et médecine), 1933.

Reeves, Hubert, *Time for Elation. Does the universe have a meaning?* (Le temps de s'enivrer. L'Univers a-t-il un sens?), du Seuil Publishers, 1985.

Schullian, D.M. and Schoen, M., *Music and Medicine*, Schumann Inc., New York, 1948.

Sivananda, Sri Swami, *Japa Yoga*, Sivananda International Center of Vedanta Yoga, 1956.

Sivananda, Sri Swami, *Music as Yoga*, Yoga-Vedanta Forest University, 1956.

Steele, D., *"Music for the Autistic Child"*, in *Music in Psychiatric Treatment*, London, 1966.

Stevens, S.S. and Warshofsky, Fred, *Sound and Listening*, Time Inc., 1966.

Tame, David, *The Secret Power of Music*, Destiny Books, 1989.

Teplov, B.M., *Psychology of Musical Aptitudes* (Psychologie des aptitudes musicales), P.U.F., Paris, 1966.

Tomatis, Pr. Alfred, *The Ear and Life* (L'Oreille et la vie), du Seuil Publishers, 1978.

Tomatis, Pr. Alfred, *The Ear and Language* (L'Oreille et le langage), du Seuil Publishers, 1978.

Tompkings, Peter, and Bird, Christopher, *The Secret Life of Plants* (La vie secrète des plantes), Robert Laffont Publishers, 1973.

Vajpeyi, Kailash, *The Science of Mantras* (La science des mantras), Guy Trédaniel Publishers, Paris, 1977.

Wall, Van de, *Music in Hospitals*, in Schullian and Schoen, 1948.

Weber, Edith, *Musicological research* (La recherche musicologique), Beauchesne Publishers, Paris, 1980.

Zonneveldt, A., *Musicotherapy with Adolescents*, Acta Paedopsychiatry, Switzerland, 1969.

216